ARMY ON ITS KNEES

DYNAMICS OF GREAT COMMISSION PRAYER

JANET MUNN

AND

STEPHEN COURT

Salvation Books
The Salvation Army International Headquarters
London, United Kingdom

ISBN 978-0-85412-842-6

Cover design by Berni Georges
Project editors: Major David Dalziel
and Paul Mortlock

Unless stated otherwise, Scripture references are taken from
the Holy Bible, New International Version,
Copyright © 1979, 1984, 2011 by Biblica,
formerly International Bible Society
Revised and updated 2011 by Hodder & Stoughton

Other Scripture references from;
AB: Amplified Bible
KJV: King James Version
NASB: New American Standard Bible
NEB: New English Bible
NIRV: New International Reader's Version
NIV 1984: New International Version 1984
NKJV: New King James Version
NLT: New Living Translation
TM: The Message
TNIV: Today's New International Version

Quotes from *The Salvation Army Song Book* (*SASB*)
are from the 1986 edition

SALVATION BOOKS

Published by Salvation Books
The Salvation Army International Headquarters
101 Queen Victoria Street, London EC4V 4EH, United Kingdom

Printed and bound by CPI Group (UK) Ltd, Croydon, CR0 4YY

WHILE I would be quick to endorse the combined work of Lieut-Colonel Janet Munn and Major Stephen Court simply on the basis of their significant contribution to the Kingdom of God and their holy living, I find myself drawn to this book of prayer. *Army On Its Knees* is an answer to prayer. I believe God is saying to us in these pages, look no further for strategies to win the world for Jesus. The strategy is prayer. This work will become a touchstone in our movement and one that will advantage the seeker and the prayer group looking for direction towards the presence of God. Hallelujah!
Commissioner Jim Knaggs, USA Western Territory

IT has been thrilling to see the way that 24-7 Prayer has spread through the worldwide ranks of The Salvation Army, galvanising fresh faith, renewing corps, and calling this great mission movement back to its roots at the intersection between the Great Commission and the Great Commandment: to love the Lord with all we have. *Army On Its Knees* is both an exciting testimony to the power of prayer, and a call to arms for this new generation.
Pete Greig, Co-founder, 24-7 Prayer and Director of Prayer, Alpha International

AS a young Christian I loved to pray, and as I did I discovered that God truly answers prayer! Now, over 35 years later I still love to pray! I was greatly encouraged and blessed when I read *Army On Its Knees*. You will be too. It is full of inspiration, encouragement and Scripture. Your prayer life will be stirred for sure. *Army On Its Knees* is a great read!
Patricia King, Founder of XP Media and Everlasting Love

ARE you serious about Jesus? God instructs us to love the Lord with all our hearts. Are you serious about reaching all kinds of people with the transformative gospel of the Lord Jesus Christ? God instructs us to love our neighbours as ourselves. If you're serious about these you must become serious about prayer. And the teaching in *Army On Its Knees* will arm you to extravagantly express and effectively exercise that two-fold love as you fight as a soldier in God's Army.
Stacey and Wesley Campbell, RevivalNOW! Ministries, revivalnow.com

DEDICATION

TO all the intercessors involved in the 200 or more 24-7 prayer rooms in the USA Eastern Territory and the War Rooms in Edmonton and Vancouver, and to the countless others joining in the Global Call to 24-7 Prayer.

'And will not God bring about justice for his chosen ones, who cry out to him day and night? Will he keep putting them off? I tell you, he will see that they get justice, and quickly. However, when the Son of Man comes, will he find faith on the earth?' Luke 18:7-8

CONTENTS

ACKNOWLEDGEMENTS

WE are grateful to those who have modelled great commission prayer for us. These include Ruth and Ian Gillingham, Patricia King, Stacey and Wesley Campbell, Richard Munn and Danielle Strickland.

We are also indebted to the teachers who have inspired us in prayer, such as Commissioner Samuel Logan Brengle, E.M. Bounds, Dutch Sheets, Richard Foster, Lieut-Colonel Damon Rader (OF) and Pete Greig of 24-7 Prayer.

Thanks to Generals Shaw Clifton and Linda Bond for calling the worldwide Salvation Army to prayer, Lieut-Colonel Richard Munn for his section on 'Circles of Influence' and to Nealson Munn for his painstaking editing.

Thanks, also, to Lieut-Colonel Laurie Robertson, Major David Dalziel and Paul Mortlock at International Headquarters, for seeing this project through to completion.

FOREWORD

THERE is across the world a growing awareness that prayer – urgent, persistent and believing prayer – is at the heart of the Great Salvation War. 'Prayer is not an adjunct to mission,' observed the missionary statesman, Paul S. Rees, 'It *is* mission!' Ours is not a calm and private faith. We are drawn ineluctably into a life-and-death struggle. The Apostle Paul understood this: 'I urge you, brothers and sisters, by our Lord Jesus Christ and by the love of the Spirit, to join me in my struggle by praying to God for me' (Romans 15:30 *Today's New International Version*). He knew that the outcome of the spiritual battles raging about him was dependent on the faithful intercessions of his network of praying 'allies' who joined him in the fight.

Nothing was more heartening to us as international leaders than the assurance of Salvationists all over the world that they were praying faithfully for us. Paul worked intentionally at establishing a network of prayer that connected him with intercessors wherever he went. 'Pray in the Spirit,' he pleaded, 'on all occasions with all kinds of prayers and requests. With this in mind, be alert and always keep on praying for all the Lord's people. Pray also for me…' (Ephesians 6:18-19 *TNIV*).

The authors of this invaluable guide for 'prayer warriors' have taken this to heart. They have been aggressively motivating, mobilizing and training Salvationists for this vital ministry of intercession. What they share here has been born and bathed in their own practice of prayer. It breathes their passion for prayer as intercession and intervention in the battle for souls. They are catalysts in a global revival of commitment to prayer that makes a difference. Some call it PUSH praying – Praying Until Something Happens!

Which of us does not resonate with the plea of the disciples, 'Master, teach us to pray'?

What follows in these pages will motivate us to fresh venturing into the life of prayer. There is guidance in prayer as a devotional discipline, understanding that effective praying rises out of the reality of our relationship with the Father and the Son, by the Spirit. For it is the Spirit who helps us in our intercessions even when we find ourselves incapable of more than 'wordless groans' (Romans 8:26 *TNIV*).

The Spirit grants to those who pray a sensitive awareness of the weaknesses and failures of others. But as Oswald Chambers observes, 'Discernment is God's call to intercession, never to fault-finding.'

Here is a call to engage in spiritual warfare through prayer. Some will be called to a lonely level of discipline in prayer. The Spirit is drawing many into such a sacrificial, and sometimes risky, life of prayer. Most will want to join forces in prayer. There are new networks of prayer forming, prayer fellowships, revivals of continuous 24-7 prayer and concerts of prayer bringing together those who agree in faith on common objectives as they pray. Does all this smack of using God – exploiting our access to the throne? The Father welcomes it. The Lord Jesus purchased that access through his own blood (Hebrews 10:19-22). The battle is his battle. The cause is his own. He welcomes us as 'workers together with him' – partners in mission through prayer.

Before the face of our Holy God there is awakened within us a passion for holiness – for clean hands and a pure heart as we approach the blood-sprinkled mercy seat. And as holy hands are lifted to the Father, he delights to act on our behalf.

Army On Its Knees is not intended to be just another pleasant read. It calls for our response. 'I implore you by our Lord Jesus Christ and by the love that the Spirit inspires, be my allies in the fight; pray…' (Romans 15:30 *New English Bible*). This was Paul's plea and it is the burden of the authors of this challenging book. More, it is an invitation to share in the ministry of Jesus, our Great Intercessor and Heavenly Captain.

Neglecting prayer, we cease to fight;
Prayer makes the soldier's armour bright;
And Satan trembles when he sees
The weakest saints upon their knees.
William Cowper
The Song Book of The Salvation Army (*SASB*) No 646 v3 alt

Retired General Paul A. Rader **and** ***Commissioner Kay F. Rader***
Lexington, Kentucky, USA

CHAPTER 1
Marching on its knees

'"An army marches on its stomach." *"C'est la soupe qui fait le soldat."* These Napoleonic aphorisms have been increasingly appreciated by our War Office.'[1]
The Windsor Magazine, January 1904

NAPOLEON famously claimed, 'An army marches on its stomach'. Years later, the missionary John 'Praying' Hyde (1865-1912) would insist that although an earthly army marches on its stomach, a spiritual army marches on its knees.

Just as an earthly army cannot prevail without food, a spiritual army cannot prevail without prayer. Soup strengthens soldiers who combat earthly forces; prayer strengthens soldiers who combat demons and sin.

Imagine an *army on its knees*: an army of dedicated, disciplined warriors advancing in humble, God-honouring obedience to the Lord Jesus Christ; an army determined to prevail against sin, the devil and despair; an army determined to win the world for Jesus.

How?

'Tackle hard, tackle low, tackle often.'

On the blistery cold day of 4 December 1909, before the battle that would decide the first Grey Cup football champion, University of Toronto Varsity Blues' Coach H.A. 'Harry' Griffiths gave a short motivational speech.

'Tackle hard, tackle low, tackle often.'

Sometimes we get ahead of ourselves. We look at the superstars of Christianity and want to be like them. Well, we want the results. We want the big crowds. We want the power. We don't notice what took place for years to produce those results, the crowds, that power. We love that in

Genesis chapter 41 Joseph was in a strategic authoritative position to affect nations during a historic drought, famine, but sometimes overlook the fact that his character had been refined for years in some of the most difficult, challenging circumstances. We desire the crowds that a certain church experienced in North America during a move of God, but most of us don't know that its leaders invested every morning – all morning – in prayer for years before this 'sudden' move of God. We admire that Brother Yun speaks around the world about the power of God in his life, but do we choose to forget that he was tortured, imprisoned and persecuted on the way to that power?

Sometimes we are enamoured with the tactics and neglect the strategies. If we provide high quality fair trade coffee after our Sunday gatherings, if we stick name tags on the volunteer parking attendants and ushers, if we ask guests to fill in visitor cards, if we follow them up with freshly baked bread within 48 hours, if we sing the latest songs, if we use the latest multimedia equipment, if we decorate the hall a certain way, *then* we'll get the outcomes we so desperately desire. Or so we think.

Sometimes we are distracted by the trivial and forget the important. Style, accent, clothing, hair – they more easily get our attention than purity, integrity and self-discipline.

Sometimes we get fixated on the advanced and the mystical at the expense of the basics. We want to know biblical Greek *and* speak in tongues. We want to preach like Martin Luther King or Catherine Booth and sing like Darlene Zschech or our favourite worship leaders. These people invested their lives to enjoy the proficiency they enjoy.

What has this to do with the first ever Grey Cup game?

Griffiths could have emphasised the special game plan, the historic significance of the match, the climax to the season, the key players on the other side of the ball, the crowd, weather conditions (2 °C, five miles per hour wind, cloudy sky, for the 2.30pm kick-off), the emotions, the challenge...

Instead, he briefly reminded the Varsity Blues of the basics – 'tackle hard, tackle low, tackle often.' If you do that, you'll win. The team followed Griffiths's instructions and secured the first of three consecutive Grey Cups.

Is it too facile to suggest that the same basics applied spiritually will guarantee spiritual success? Does it sound too easy to suggest we need to exhort each other to pray hard, pray long, pray often? We're not persuaded.

We believe that the basics provide a foundation. We believe that enduring, intimate, extraordinary prayer generates spiritual power, advance and victory. We believe that God has invited us into relationship with him and, more than that, fellowship. We will not settle with a formal relationship that confirms his fatherhood in our lives and our inheritance in his Kingdom, as amazing as that is. We want the fellowship that he also offers and desires – we hunger for companionship with the King.

It is this enduring, intimate, extraordinary prayer – pray hard, pray long, pray often – that sustains communion with God, that drives the salvation war, that guarantees personal victory over sin and corporate victory over the devil.

What does it look like? Well, for the early-risers in Korea sometimes it looks like chaos, with everyone up and about and praying out loud at the same time. In our more charismatic presentations it looks like a multitude of palms faced heavenward in worship. Amongst the more contemplative of our brothers and sisters, it can look like solitary silence for long periods. Some of our primitives can be seen circling a room praying the Bible out loud to God.

Fervour comes in different forms. Zeal appears in a variety of shapes and sizes. Diligence manifests itself in many ways.

To equip you to win the world for Jesus, this book describes the fundamentals of prayer, from private prayer to missional prayer. However, these pages are not intended merely to inform. They are also intended to inspire – to inspire you to deploy the power of prayer in the battle for the realisation of the Great Commission. Remember, as a soldier in a spiritual army you are engaged in a battle which has eternal consequences.

The Lord Jesus Christ, the Commander of this Army, is coming soon. He has deployed us to fight and to win. Approach these pages as a mission training guide that shows you the 'whys' and the 'hows' of prayer, the key to spiritually gaining ground personally and the means of advancing the great global salvation warfare.

Use it as a prayer manual to have in your hands while you pray, to help you pray. Use it in the prayer room. Pray through its pages – on your knees.

This Army marches on its knees. So pray hard, pray long, pray often.

[1] *The Windsor Magazine*, January, Ward Lock & Co., 1904.

CHAPTER 2

Fullness: the best is yet to come

What are your expectations in prayer?

'YOU have been given fullness in Christ, who is the head over every power and authority.'

Colossians 2:10 *New International Version 1984*

Slowly sinks the reign of darkness,
Yielding to the Saviour's day,
When the slaves of sinful bondage
Cast their evil chains away.
Upward, Christward, homeward, Godward!
Millions who are now afar
Shall be brought into the Kingdom,
Where the Father's children are.

Albert Orsborn *SASB* No 776 v 2

'He will not let your foot slip –
He who watches over you will not slumber;
Indeed, he who watches over Israel
will neither slumber nor sleep.'

Psalm 121:3-4

Have you ever thought that the Lord may already have used up all his best miracles? That the great things he has already done for heroes in the Bible and throughout the history of the people of God are all that he has to offer?

Janet's grandmother described to her how she had experienced some powerful prayer meetings with The Salvation Army in Canada, but that was in 1915! Sometimes people talk as though God was only actively at work, only doing powerful deeds, back in the good old days. Certainly, God, the Ancient of Days, has been around a long time and has done some amazing things through the centuries. And it is true that a lot of the best stories of his works are from a long time ago.

Yet from the beginning the Lord planned for a progressive, cumulative increase in the knowledge of God on the earth. We see similar principles in the natural realm all the time. Scientists don't start their research over again with each generation, but rather build on the discoveries of previous generations. This is true in medicine, the arts, communications, transportation, and so on. One generation builds upon and adds to what their forebears have experienced and discovered. This is true also of the reality of God on the earth. 'Increase' has been a key word since God's first instruction to Adam and Eve, when he told them to 'be fruitful and *increase*' (Genesis 1:22, our italics). God repeatedly promised increase to the Israelites through Moses, through Jeremiah and through Ezekiel. In the infant Church, too, there was evidence of increase, as 'the word of God continued to increase and spread' (Acts 12:24 *NIV 1984*).

Increase – toward what? Read what Habakkuk wrote: 'For as the waters fill the sea, the earth will be filled with an awareness of the glory of the Lord' (Habakkuk 2:14 *New Living Translation*).

That's where the earth is headed! All this increase – in knowledge, in technology, in communications, in population – is increase leading to a time of fullness, in the fullness of time.

Fullness of Salvation

Full salvation, full salvation,
Lo! the fountain, opened wide,
Streams through every land and nation
From the Saviour's wounded side!
Full salvation, full salvation,
Streams an endless crimson tide.

Francis Bottome *SASB* No 540 v 1

> 'What makes us think we can escape if we ignore this great salvation?'
>
> Hebrews 2:3 *NLT*

Pie in the sky? In the sweet by and by? Someday when I die?

No way! We want it all, we want it now – and so should you. When asked how to pray, Jesus didn't teach his friends to pray, 'Lord, just help me to hang on 'til Heaven, when I'll get my reward, and be freed from this misery, and be healed and delivered and holy.' Rather, he taught them boldly to *declare* (the gist of the language of 'the Lord's Prayer'): Father, about your kingdom...*come!* And regarding your will...*be done!* Right here, right now, on earth, in this age, in our lifetimes, in exactly the same way as your will is being done in Heaven! Now that's praying for fullness in Christ – which, after all, is what Jesus suffered to provide for us.

The things Jesus bore and suffered are described in various translations of Isaiah 53:4-5 as 'griefs', 'sorrows', 'sicknesses', 'diseases', 'infirmities', 'iniquities' and 'transgressions' – the full list of human afflictions and miseries. The full range of brokenness was unleashed upon the Messiah and he bore it all, to the full. This sounds like the price of *full* salvation. We want it all, we want it now, and so should you. After all, the full price has been paid for the fullness of our salvation.

'When evening came, many who were demon-possessed were brought to him, and he drove out the spirits with a word and healed all the sick. This was to fulfil what was spoken through the prophet Isaiah: "He took up our infirmities and bore our diseases"' (Matthew 8:16-17).

Fullness through Emptiness

> 'Does God call you? ...Go and God will be with you...and as the years speed by you will increasingly thank God that no business prospects, no fond friendships, no lust of power or love of secluded ease kept you from the battle's front with its burdens and bitter conflicts and fierce sorrows and soul-satisfying triumphs.'
>
> Samuel Logan Brengle, *Heart Talks on Holiness*

'Then Jesus said to his disciples, "If any of you wants to be my follower, you must turn from your selfish ways, take up your cross, and follow me. If you try to hang on to your life, you will lose it. But if you give up your life for my sake, you will save it."'

Matthew 16:24-25 *NLT*

There is something in human beings that welcomes, desires and seeks out discipline, challenge, self-sacrifice and even suffering, especially when these things lead to something we perceive as valuable. How else can we explain the enormous interest in reality television shows like *Survivor* and the discomfort their participants are willing to undergo?

Jesus is the ultimate example of a person willing to endure difficulties in order to obtain something he deemed valuable. He laid aside the mighty power and glory due only to God, becoming fully human, in frail flesh, vulnerable to human cruelty, hatred and violence, as is manifest vividly at the crucifixion. And for what? The Apostle Paul reminds us in Philippians that because of Christ's self-sacrifice, because of his endurance, God the Father has exalted Jesus to the highest place, where he is now and forever worshipped and honoured in the throne room of God, and that ultimately everyone will recognize and acknowledge his honoured position. But that is not the reason for which Jesus Christ suffered. We are.

We are the reward, the highly valued prize for which Jesus suffered. We are his inheritance. We are what he died for. We are Christ's reward. Amazingly, the motivation behind his self-emptying was us.

Now consider this: 'Your attitude should be the same as that of Christ Jesus' (Philippians 2:5 *NIV 1984*).

And this: 'Peter said to him, "We have left all we had to follow you!" "I tell you the truth," Jesus said to them, "no one who has left home or wife or brothers or parents or children for the sake of the kingdom of God will fail to receive many times as much in this age and, in the age to come, eternal life"' (Luke 18:28-30).

Keep that in heart when you struggle with persevering, extraordinary prayer on your knees and when under enemy attack or worldly distraction or physical weariness.

Intergenerational Fullness

'Day by day you must labour to wake up your children to the realisation that they belong to God, and that he has sent them into the world, not to look after their own little petty, personal interests, but to devote themselves to the promotion of his, and that in doing this they will find happiness, usefulness and glory.'

Catherine Booth, *The Highway of Our God*

'His preaching will turn the hearts of fathers to their children, and the hearts of children to their fathers.'

Malachi 4:6 *NLT*

'She's a chip off the old block.' 'The acorn doesn't fall far from the tree.' 'Like father, like son.' All these sayings remind us that the generations are interconnected.

Proverbs reminds us that the connection can be both delightful and painful: 'To have a fool for a son brings grief; there is no joy for the father of a fool' (17:21), and regarding the virtuous woman: 'Her children arise and call her blessed' (31:28 *NIV 1984*).

Psalm 78 tells us that the Lord intends for one generation to pass on the knowledge of God to the next. This is his design. If ever there was a series of interconnected generations it was the Hebrew patriarchs – Abraham, Isaac and Jacob. God often describes himself as their God, the tri-generational God, the God of the generations, the God of Abraham, Isaac and Jacob.

For these nomadic, desert-dwelling people, access to a well was essential to survival. Before Isaac, Abraham had dug wells in the desert, which Isaac eventually re-dug. 'Isaac reopened the wells that had been dug in the time of his father Abraham, which the Philistines had stopped up after Abraham died, and he gave them the same names his father had given them' (Genesis 26:18). Wells were life-saving and life-giving. Isaac knew this, so he re-dug his father's wells, which was much easier than digging his own.

A converse yet complementary theme running throughout Scripture is the younger generation's importance to the older generation. Discussing this in the Gospels, Jesus turns our expectations upside down. He makes statements like: 'I tell you the truth, anyone who will not receive the Kingdom of God like a little child will never enter it' (Luke 18:17) and 'Whoever welcomes a little child like this in my name welcomes me' (Matthew 18:5 *NIV 1984*).

Jesus, the only begotten son of the uncreated God, likens himself to a little child in our midst!

Fullness: the Promise of Greater Things

What a work the Lord has done
By his saving grace;
Let us praise him, every one,
In his holy place.
He has saved us gloriously,
Led us onward faithfully,
Yet he promised we should see
Even greater things.

Greater things! Greater things!
Give us faith, O Lord, we pray,
Faith for greater things.
Albert Orsborn *SASB* No 769 v 1

'God had provided something better for us, so that apart from us they would not be made perfect.'
Hebrews 11:40 *New American Standard Bible*

I [Janet] have some extremely competitive people in my extended family. This competitiveness is expressed in maxims like: 'Winning isn't the main thing, it's the only thing!' In a 'friendly' game of two-on-two basketball, blows and injuries are dismissed with a manly shout of 'No autopsy, no foul!'

The New Testament's authors aren't that competitive, but it's striking that the writer of the book of Hebrews uses the word 'better' more than 10 times in comparing the old covenant to the new. God the Father, through Jesus Christ, has provided a better hope (7:19), a better covenant (7:22), better promises (8:6), better sacrifices (9:23), better possessions (10:34), a better country (11:16), a better resurrection (11:35) and, in summary, just a big 'something better for us' (11:40)!

Likewise, in 2 Corinthians 3:2-3 Paul contrasts the letter written on tablets of stone with the letter written on the tablet of the heart. The old covenant was of the letter that kills, the new is of the Spirit that gives life. That death-bringing ministry, through Moses, still came with glory, fading though it was. How much more glorious is the ministry of the Spirit!

'If the ministry that condemns men is glorious, *how much more* glorious is the ministry that brings righteousness! For what was glorious *has no glory now in comparison* with the surpassing glory. And if what was fading away came with glory, *how much greater is the glory* of that which lasts!' (2 Corinthians 3:9-11 *NIV 1984* – our italics).

'And we, who with unveiled faces all reflect the Lord's glory, are being transformed into his likeness with *ever-increasing glory*, which comes from the Lord, who is the Spirit' (2 Corinthians 3:18 *NIV 1984*, our italics).

These verses are a reminder that we have not yet plumbed the depths of the fullness of Christ in our day.

'Now to him who is able to do immeasurably more than all we ask or imagine, according to his power that is at work within us, to him be glory in the church and in Christ Jesus throughout all generations, for ever and ever! Amen' (Ephesians 3:20-21).

Our humble, sacrificial adoration and intercession is empowered by his power at work within us! He himself has already given us the power required for the answers to our requests, for the revelation desired in our entreaties, for the perspective helpful in our uncertainties, for the zeal essential to our endurance, for the fear of the Lord crucial to our sanctification.

International Fullness

O boundless salvation! deep ocean of love,
O fulness of mercy, Christ brought from above,
The whole world redeeming, so rich and so free,
Now flowing for all men, come, roll over me!
William Booth *SASB* No 298 v 1

'But you will receive power when the Holy Spirit comes upon you. And will be my witnesses, telling people about me everywhere – in Jerusalem, throughout Judea, in Samaria, and to the ends of the earth.'
Acts 1:8 *NLT*

'It is not good for the man to be alone' (Genesis 2:18). Aloneness is the first aspect of God's creation described in Genesis as 'not good'. Distressed babies often just want to be held, nothing more. The sick, the lonely, even the dying, are deeply comforted just by having someone else present with them. We need each other. Our need for community is deep, universal and God-given. Alone: not good. In community: very good.

In the beginning there was the Father, the Son and the Holy Spirit – the first community, the perfect community. The life in the godhead could not be contained, but had to spill out in the beauty and extravagance of creation, including the creation of a larger community that included humanity. God's intention was for humankind to share in this perfect community. The divine mandate that human beings 'be fruitful and multiply, fill the earth and subdue it' was meant to expand the community more and more, family by family, generation by generation, filling the earth with the ever-expanding community of God.

God continued to expand the 'circle of inclusion' through the Hebrew people, beginning with Abram, to whom God promised, 'I will bless you…and *all the peoples of the earth* will be blessed through you' (Genesis 12:2-3, our italics). Jesus Christ commissioned and empowered his Church to go as witnesses to all nations, making disciples as they went – from Jerusalem, Judea and Samaria and to the ends of the earth.

This God-community seems hungry for more, always reaching, stretching, growing, expanding and embracing in joyful love. At the end of human history those gathered around the throne of God are from all nations; every tribe, language, people and race are present. This is and always has been the heart of God; all people; all nations; every language; every race all gathered to himself. God is a happy father celebrating having his children home for the holidays, a joyful bridegroom delighting in the beauty of the bride for whom he has long waited and prepared.

This is the fullness of the redemption of the world for which Christ died. Nothing else will do. William Booth saw the heavenly vision: 'fullness of mercy', 'the whole world redeeming', 'now flowing for all'.

'He is the atoning sacrifice for our sins, and not only for ours but also for the sins of the whole world' (1 John 2:2). How bolstering is this truth to our praying? We know first-hand of his efficacy in our own lives and that same power and sacrifice is for the whole world! It is not only his will but his capacity to answer our ambitious prayers. Our international prayers are more than matched by his global atonement.

Persevere for Fullness

> 'Do you know what you have to do to backslide? Absolutely nothing.'
>
> J. Donald Freese

> 'You don't have to see God to know him. Faith, which works by love, can see in the dark.'
>
> Lyell M. Rader

> 'Then Jesus told his disciples a parable to show them that they should always pray and not give up.'
>
> Luke 18:1

Long before a woman even appears pregnant, let alone gives birth, there is life growing within her.

To take another example, think of all those hours spent memorizing vocabulary and conjugating verbs, only to feel (still) completely bewildered by a foreign language. Gradually, however, the riddles are unravelled; the babble becomes sensible; the language becomes comprehensible.

So it is with prayer – with great determination, pressing on, not giving up, always believing, with earnest and deep heart cries, sometimes even after years of seeing nothing change, one waits patiently and then, suddenly – breakthrough! In a moment the miracle comes. She is healed, delivered, rescued. He is brought to his senses. After all those years, after a long battle, abruptly but finally, victory comes. Something was happening all along. What took so long? What if we'd given up?

Jesus repeatedly described the Kingdom of Heaven as like a seed, or a farmer who plants a seed and waters it consistently, not knowing how it grows, although it surely does. Imperceptible yet real growth is happening in the seed cared for by the farmer and in the Kingdom of God when God's people pray.

In 1 Kings 18:1 we read that when God told Elijah it was going to rain after three and a half years of drought, the downpour was not immediate. Elijah heard the promise of God but first faced a fierce battle – a confrontation with the prophets of Baal. Immediately after the battle, Elijah began to speak God's promises, even to King Ahab.

Elijah crouched down with his head between his knees and began to travail, to labour in prayer, helping to birth the purposes and promises of God on the earth. Seven times he asked his servant to check the sky for clouds. The first six times they saw nothing, not a cloud in the sky. But Elijah persevered and on the seventh time, the seventh 'push', the promise was born. Elijah's servant reported: 'A cloud as small as a man's hand is rising from the sea' (1 Kings 18:44).

In Luke 18, Jesus taught his disciples to pray always and never give up.

The evil one fears our perseverance. He fears our focus, because when we are determined to persevere in prayer according to the Word of the Lord, our breakthrough is sure. That is why the pressure becomes so intense sometimes – the devil wants us to stop.

Never give up. '[Love] always protects, always trusts, always hopes, *always perseveres*' (1 Corinthians 13:7, our italics).

Prayer Group Guide

- How are you experiencing fullness in your praying community?
- How might you make your praying community more fully characterized by fullness?
- How can you spread the experience of fullness through your praying?

CHAPTER 3
Intercession: called to persevere in prayer

Introduction

FOR a useful exploration of the subject of intercession, we recommend Dutch Sheets's wonderful book *Intercessory Prayer*. This chapter is inspired in part by his teaching.

Is prayer really necessary? John Wesley thought so: 'God does nothing in this world except in response to believing prayer.'

Psalm 25:14: 'The Lord *confides* in those who fear him; he makes his covenant known to them' (our italics).

Do we really believe this? Do we really believe that the Lord Almighty – Yahweh, God of angel armies – will confide in people like us? Or do we think, perhaps even subconsciously, that because of God's sovereignty and omnipotence, our prayer doesn't matter? What does Scripture tell us about the role of intercessory prayer in the relationship between the sovereign God and weak, frail humanity?

'Ask the Lord for rain in the springtime' (Zechariah 10:1). This verse counsels us that we should not hesitate to turn to God in our times of need. God is our provider and he wants us to rely on him.

The Lord tells us to pray for his Kingdom to come and to ask the Lord of the harvest to call forth labourers. But doesn't he want to do these things anyway? Why must we ask for daily bread when he already knows our needs? Is it possible that our asking somehow 'releases' him to respond?

We need to know why we should pray in order to stay motivated to do so. To that end, here is a principle to remember: God is a God of relationship. *He is training us to reign with him.*

Genesis 1:26-28 (*NIV 1984*): 'Then God said, "Let us make man in our image, in our likeness, and let them rule over the fish of the sea and the birds of the air, over the livestock, over all the earth, and over all the creatures that move along the ground." So God created man in his own image, in the image of God he created him; male and female he created them. God blessed them and said to them, "Be fruitful and increase in number; fill the earth and subdue it. Rule over the fish of the sea and the birds of the air and over every living creature that moves on the ground."'

> 'When I consider your heavens,
> the work of your fingers,
> the moon and the stars,
> which you have set in place,
> what are mere mortals that you are mindful of them,
> human beings that you care for them?
> You have made them a little lower than the heavenly beings
> and crowned them with glory and honour.
> You made them rulers over the works of your hands;
> you put everything under their feet:
> all flocks and herds,
> and the animals of the wild,
> the birds in the sky,
> and the fish in the sea,
> all that swim the paths of the seas.'
> Psalm 8:3-8 (*TNIV*)

We are made in God's 'image', 'shadow', or 'likeness'. This reality seems almost impossible to comprehend and yet we must do so if we are to appreciate God's love and purposes for us. Adam was similar to God, modelled and shaped after him to such an extent that God said, 'There's nothing I can compare humans to but me.'

Humanity is the pinnacle of God's creation. What a mind-boggling thought! Hallelujah. God's expansive, creative, inclusive love resulted in the creation of a family – people to whom he could relate, people who think like him, people who would become his sons and daughters.

He wanted humans to have dominion here on earth – to rule, to put things under our feet: 'You're in charge. You look like me, now rule over my creation for me.'

Psalm 8:5: 'You crowned [humanity] with *glory* and honour' (our italics). 'Glory' is a translation of the Hebrew word *kabod*, which connotes weightiness. God is saying, 'I invest you with the weight of my glory. You are carrying a lot of weight around here! I want to be recognisable in you.' In addition to glory and 'weightiness', *kabod* further suggests abundance, riches and splendour – see 2 Corinthians 4:17. Profound.

And that is just the 'glory' part! God has given us a second crown, one of honour – *hadar*, also translated 'majesty'. Hallelujah!

He not only crowns us with glory and honour; he also shines on us so brightly that we reflect his glory: 'And we, who with unveiled faces all reflect the Lord's glory, are being transformed into his likeness with ever-increasing glory, which comes from the Lord, who is the Spirit' (2 Corinthians 3:18). This leaves us in a predicament. Although we are made in God's image, we must be changed, because through sin we've fallen short of the glory of God.

As we understand 'glory' as implying God's presence recognisably manifest, what does it mean to say that God 'crowned' us with glory? It means that God created us to be recognized as him on earth – to be his re-presentation, his representatives. Humans are to 'present again' God's will and God's ways.

God says, 'I want you to rule on the earth – to rule, to reign, to govern, to represent, to manage': 'The highest heavens belong to the Lord, but the earth he has given to humankind' (Psalm 115:16 *TNIV*).

So God delegated the governance of the earth to people.

God Works through Prayer

God's transfer of earthly authority to humans was so complete that we, in turn, were able to give it to someone else – namely, Satan. Consider that startling concept. God was so committed to the principle of re-presentation that he delegated sufficient authority to humans for them to sell, give away, lose, or trade that same authority!

God wasn't pretending, the way a parent might pretend to allow a small child to drive a car. After seeing our mistakes, our sin, our misuse of our authority, he did not take back the steering wheel. Our dominion of the earth is no game. The stakes are high.

Unfortunately, Adam and Eve allowed Satan to usurp authority over the earth. Even Jesus called Satan 'the ruler of this world'. He's also known as 'the prince of this world': 'Now is the time for judgement on this world; now the prince of this world will be driven out' (John 12:31).

Most of us know the story of how all this transpired. After Adam and Eve, tempted by the serpent, sinned by disobeying God's instructions, God stepped in. He adjudicated between the serpent and the humans (note that Satan is properly the enemy of humans, not of the Lord – he is not even in the same league as God), explaining the ramifications of their sin: 'And I will put enmity between you and the woman, and between your offspring and hers; he will crush your head, and you will strike his heel' (Genesis 3:15).

A human gave away our authority, so a human had to take it back. And that is what Jesus did.

What are we to make of this? Most Christians enthusiastically accept Jesus' divinity. But why was it necessary for Jesus also to be fully man?

Jesus' humanity positioned him perfectly to engage the enemy. In Matthew 8:29, demons recognize Jesus' divinity: 'Son of God…Have you come here to torment us before the appointed time?' (*Amplified Bible*). In Mark 5:7, they fall before Jesus and cry out, 'Son of the Most High God? I implore you by God, do not torment me!' (*NASB*).

So a demon is calling on God to spare him from Jesus! How do we explain this strange episode? The demons knew that they had assumed authority over the earth after the tragic incident in Eden (Genesis chapter 3). They also knew that Jesus, in his divinity, was coming eventually to retake the earth, but that the time for this final cataclysm had not yet come. That's why they sought God's intervention.

What they didn't know was that Jesus of Nazareth was not only fully divine, but also fully human. That is why he had a right to intervene. A human gave authority to Satan and a human had arrived to reclaim that authority (see James Garlow's *The Covenant: A Study of God's Extraordinary Love for You*[2]). It is for this reason that Jesus became incarnate as a human.

Scripture reinforces this teaching: 'Therefore, just as sin entered the world through one man, and death through sin, and in this way death came to all men, because all sinned…if, by the trespass of the one man, death reigned through that one man, how much more will those who receive God's abundant provision of grace and of the gift of righteousness reign in life through the one man, Jesus Christ' (Romans 5:12,17).

'For since death came through a man, the resurrection of the dead comes also through a man. For as in Adam all die, so in Christ all will be made alive. But each in his own turn: Christ, the firstfruits; then, when he comes, those who belong to him' (1 Corinthians 15:21-23).

'So it is written: "The first man Adam became a living being"; the last Adam, a life-giving spirit' (1 Corinthians 15:45).

God had to become one of us, a human, in order to regain what Adam gave away.

Humans as God's Link to the Earth

God wants humans to invite him in, to seek his help (Zechariah 10:1). Elijah, who knew the word of God, took God up on this offer (see 1 Kings chapter 18 and James chapter 5) and asked him for rain. And it rained.

In 1 Kings 18:1, God himself extends the promise of rain to Elijah. But though this offer was God's will, God's initiative and God's timing, according to his own plan he needed a *human being* to bring rain to the earth *through* prayer.

Remarkably, Elijah still had to ask seven times before God responded! When God makes a promise to us, we are often tempted to become complacent. However, God does not announce his plan so that we can relax, but so that we can participate.

Remember Zechariah 10:1 – it is God who sends rain, but it is we who must request it. It is as if God says, 'I need your cooperation. Otherwise, I'd have finished the whole thing a long time ago.' Like Elijah, we must 'birth' God's purposes on the earth (see 1 Kings 18:41-46 and note Elijah's body language).

Look at these chapters: Daniel 9 and Jeremiah 25 and 29.

While a captive in Babylon, Daniel read Jeremiah's prophecy that the Hebrews' Babylonian captivity would last 70 years. He realized that this time was almost up. Yet Daniel did not passively wait out the end of the 70-year term. Instead, his faith was stirred by reading Jeremiah's prophecy and he began to pray that it would be fulfilled.

We do not take God's place. Jeremiah's prophecy was simply a proclamation of God's will. In Daniel, God sought a human with the heart to intercede, a human through whom to fulfil his word.

Through Humans God Works on the Earth

'Surely the Sovereign Lord does nothing without revealing his plan to his servants the prophets' (Amos 3:7).

'I looked for someone among them who would build up the wall and stand before me in the gap on behalf of the land so I would not have to destroy it, but I found no one. So I will pour out my wrath on them and consume them with my fiery anger, bringing down on their own heads all they have done, declares the Sovereign Lord' (Ezekiel 22:30-31 *TNIV*).

God is holy and just and can't ignore sin. However, he is also loving and merciful. 'I couldn't simply excuse sin. I needed someone to "stand in the gap" – then I would have forgiven.'

Does God always get his way? How many things have happened on the earth, and are still happening today, that God doesn't want?

It might seem an obvious point, but just for the record, God does not always get what he wants. In fact, history shows that events are often contrary to his plan. For example: he wants us to be free of sin, yet humanity is deeply sinful. So in this respect God's will is thwarted many, many times every day. God wants no one to perish, to be separated from him, yet many people die without ever finding him. Indeed, it might be fair to say that God rarely gets what he wants.

This is evident as early as Genesis: 'The Lord was grieved that he had made man on the earth, and his heart was filled with pain' (Genesis 6:6).

'So the Lord was sorry he had ever made them...It broke his heart' (Genesis 6:6 *NLT*).

God seeks humans – Christians – who will realize his will through prayer. God works through humans and he wants us to be his intercessors. We can be intimidated or excited by this privilege.

'Keep on asking, and you will receive what you ask for. Keep on seeking, and you will find. Keep on knocking, and the door will be opened to you. For everyone who asks, receives. Everyone who seeks, finds. And to everyone who knocks, the door will be opened' (Matthew 7:7-8 *NLT*).

God says, 'I'll tell you what to ask. You ask me and I'm going to do it.' We don't have to initiate anything; we just respond to God. Or, to adapt Jesus' testimony in John 5:19 to a prayer that we might use: 'Help us to see what you're doing and do what we're seeing.' God is the initiator. Watch how he initiates in the following verse:

'And I will pour out on the house of David and the inhabitants of Jerusalem a spirit of grace and supplication' (Zechariah 12:10).

'Then I will pour out a spirit of grace and prayer on the family of David and on the people of Jerusalem' (Zechariah 12:10 *NLT*).

Be open to receive God's spirit of grace and supplication – the spirit of intercession.

Meetings

As a teenager I [Janet] worked hard to qualify as a lifeguard. At the time I was a timid, petite young girl. Our aquatics instructor, Donny, was a bodybuilder – a big, athletic and aggressive man. He weighed twice as much as I did, was a foot taller than me and was in peak physical condition. During one training session our task was to 'rescue' Donny who, flailing about in deep water, would behave like a panic-stricken drowning victim, grasping haphazardly at anyone approaching him. I was anxious – and rightly so. Not long after I entered the pool, Donny's bulky forearm met my nose and front teeth. There was literally blood in the water. Years later I learned that my front tooth had sustained nerve damage.

A happier meeting occurred a few years later when I met my fiancé at the airport after four months of separation. He was in England, I was in Boston, USA. Before he returned to Boston I prepared to meet him. Before I went to the airport I went shopping and bought the most expensive dress I'd ever purchased. I made an appointment with a hairdresser. I wore perfume. I was ready for the reunion.

On the cross, two similarly contrasting meetings took place:

1. Satan met defeat, receiving a divine forearm to the nose and teeth. This meeting was of course one of violence and conflict, but also one of victory for the Lord. As the Psalmist wrote (3:7), 'Arise, O Lord! Deliver me, O my God! Strike all my enemies on the jaw; break the teeth of the wicked.'

2. A groom met his bride. This meeting was infused with beauty, joy and reunion. 'Husbands, love your wives, just as Christ loved the church and gave himself up for her to make her holy, cleansing her by the washing with water through the word, and to present her to himself as a radiant church, without stain or wrinkle or any other blemish, but holy and blameless' (Ephesians 5:25-27).

Two extremes! Only God could combine two such 'meetings' in a single event. God says, 'I will meet with you. You can meet with me. Through our meeting the enemy will meet defeat.' That's intercession.

Jesus' sacrifice was a divinely arranged meeting between God and humans. The mystery and beauty of such reconciliation in the spiritual realm is evidenced in Psalm 85:10: 'Love and faithfulness meet together; righteousness and peace kiss each other.' As intercessors, we have the wonderful responsibility to bring about reconciliation – just as God the Father did with us through Christ: 'All this is from God, who reconciled us to himself through Christ and gave us the ministry of reconciliation' (2 Corinthians 5:18).

God has called us to the ministry of reconciliation. He wants us to arrange for people to meet with him. When we intercede in prayer, we meet with God and ask him to meet with someone else. The father is eager to be reunited with those for whom his son died.

Persistence in Prayer

Why persist in prayer? Do we somehow talk God into things? Do we twist his arm to persuade him to do something? When we see answers, is that an indication that God has finally 'caved in'? Is he undecided until our perseverance wins his favour?

Avowedly or not, many of us are troubled by questions such as these.

We need to recognize that our prayers do more than motivate the Father to action. They release the Holy Spirit's power in us; they accomplish something directly. God exerts his strength through us when we pray. Consider these translations of James 5:16: 'Therefore, confess your sins to each other and pray for each other so that you may be healed. *The prayer of a righteous person is powerful and effective*' (*TNIV*, our italics). 'Confess your sins to each other and pray for each other so that you may be healed. *The earnest prayer of a righteous person has great power and produces wonderful results*' (*NLT*, our italics).

Of course, the power and energy of prayer are God's, not ours. We are the temple of the Holy Spirit – the Holy of Holies, the body of Christ, the place where God dwells. His power isn't confined, however, but flows outwards: 'Whoever believes in me, as the Scripture has said, streams of living water will flow from within him' (John 7:38).

Healing flows from us, bringing life to others.

Sometimes intercession is likened not to a stream but to a military battle: 'Take the helmet of salvation and the sword that the Spirit wields, which is the word [*rhema*] of God. Pray at all times (on every occasion, in every season) in the Spirit, with all [manner of] prayer and entreaty. To that end keep alert and watch with strong purpose and perseverance, interceding in behalf of all the saints (God's consecrated people)' (Ephesians 6:17-18 *AB*).

Measures of Faith

The Bible speaks of 'measures' of sin. Consider the following verse:

'In the fourth generation your descendants will come back here, for the sin of the Amorites has not yet reached its full measure' (Genesis 15:16).

But if there are measures of sin, there are also measures of grace – and, correspondingly, measures of power. We operate in a spirit opposite to that of sin and we need great grace, great power, and hence great faith, to defeat great sin.

'With great power the apostles continued to testify to the resurrection of the Lord Jesus, and much grace was upon them all' (Acts 4:33).

Measures of faith:

- No faith (Mark 4:40)
- Little faith (Matthew 8:26)
- Faith (Luke 5:20)
- Great faith (Luke 7:9)

Persevere to Fullness

There are many questions regarding unanswered prayer (*God on Mute: Engaging the Silence of Unanswered Prayer*, by Pete Greig,[3] is an excellent read on the subject) and anyone who has been praying for very long will have experienced some disappointments and been left with some unanswered questions. Yet the Scriptures teach us to persevere in prayer, encouraging believers to be persistent in prayer – in the language of Luke 18:1, to 'always pray and not give up'. Biblical examples abound:

- Elijah prayed seven times before God responded – yet his request was God's will, God's idea and God's initiative (1 Kings 18:42-44).
- Daniel prayed for 21 days before an angel appeared to him (Daniel chapter 10).
- Elijah prayed three times before life returned to the dead boy (1 Kings 17:21-24).
- Jesus anointed the blind man twice before his sight was restored (Mark 8:22-26).
- Jesus prayed for three hours in the garden before his crucifixion (Matthew 26:36-45).

Why is such perseverance necessary? Different levels of God's power are needed to accomplish different things. You wouldn't use the same amount of electricity to charge a flashlight as you would use to light an entire house.

It is only after enough power has been released through prayer that things are accomplished. In Mark chapter 6, Jesus performs no miracles and only a few healings – seemingly because God's power was blocked by unbelief.

This is why sometimes it takes time for prayers to be answered – it takes time to release enough spiritual power *to accomplish God's purposes.*

When our prayers are finally answered, God's response often seems to arrive suddenly, because before then we could not see evidence of the power our prayers released.

How, then, should we aim to develop as intercessors? Consider the cheetah: the cheetah can run at speeds of up to 70 miles an hour, but only for a few seconds, because it has a small heart. It will only capture its prey if it does so almost as soon as it bursts into motion. After just a few seconds of unsuccessful pursuit, it tires and lags.

Praying Christians, by contrast, must have stamina, not speed. Our hearts need to grow bigger. Fortunately, with God this is entirely possible: 'Now to him who is able to do immeasurably more than all we ask or imagine, according to his power that is at work within us, to him be glory in the church and in Christ Jesus throughout all generations, for ever and ever! Amen' (Ephesians 3:20-21).

The *power source* is clearly not the problem. Things happen through God's power at work in *us*, in the measure of his power operative in us.

This is a mysterious process, but Scripture gives us glimpses behind the curtain at its operation: 'And when he had taken it, the four living creatures and the twenty-four elders fell down before the Lamb. Each one had a harp and they were holding golden bowls full of incense, which are the prayers of the saints' (Revelation 5:8).

'Another angel, who had a golden censer, came and stood at the altar. He was given much incense to offer, with the prayers of all the saints, on the golden altar before the throne. The smoke of the incense, together with the prayers of the saints, went up before God from the angel's hand.

Then the angel took the censer, filled it with fire from the altar, and hurled it on the earth; and there came peals of thunder, rumblings, flashes of lightning and an earthquake' (Revelation 8:3-5).

God stores up our prayers in Heaven, mixes them with his holy fire and pours the results out on the earth. So persevere – don't give up. Agree with fellow believers – multiply the power of prayer. The emphasis is not on huge numbers but on the power of agreement. For example:

- 'How could one man chase a thousand, or two put ten thousand to flight, unless their Rock had sold them, unless the Lord had given them up?' (Deuteronomy 32:30).
- 'A thousand will flee at the threat of one; at the threat of five you will all flee away, till you are left life a flagstaff on a mountaintop, like a banner on a hill' (Isaiah 30:17).

May God open our eyes to see what is happening in the heavenly realms when we pray.

Principles of Prayer

We conclude this chapter with a look at five 'principles of prayer': scriptural principles to bear in mind whenever you come before God's throne. They are:

1. *Pneuma*
2. Promises
3. Passion
4. Presence
5. Persistence

1. *Pneuma* – the Greek word *pneuma* means 'breath', 'wind' or 'spirit'. This is the word used in Ephesians 6:18: 'And *pray in the Spirit* on all occasions with all kinds of prayers and requests. With this in mind, be alert and always keep on praying for all the saints' (our italics).

2. Promises – because God has revealed himself in his Word, we don't have to guess at his will. Remember what Jesus says in John

15:15: 'I no longer call you servants, because a servant does not know his master's business. Instead, I have called you friends, for everything that I learned from my Father I have made known to you.'

3. Passion – 'During the days of Jesus' life on earth, he offered up prayers and petitions with loud cries and tears to the one who could save him from death, and he was heard because of his reverent submission' (Hebrews 5:7).

'Don't burn out; keep yourselves fueled and aflame. Be alert servants of the Master, cheerfully expectant. Don't quit in hard times; pray all the harder' (Romans 12:11-12 *The Message*).

4. Presence – 'For where two or three come together in my name, there am I with them' (Matthew 18:20).

5. Persistence – 'Then Jesus told his disciples a parable to show them that they should always pray and not give up' (Luke 18:1).

Finally, let's remember Paul's triumphant benediction in Ephesians 3:14-21:

'For this reason I kneel before the Father, from whom every family in Heaven and on earth derives its name. I pray that out of his glorious riches he may strengthen you with power through his Spirit in your inner being, so that Christ may dwell in your hearts through faith. And I pray that you, being rooted and established in love, may have power, together with all the Lord's holy people, to grasp how wide and long and high and deep is the love of Christ, and to know this love that surpasses knowledge – that you may be filled to the measure of all the fullness of God. Now to him who is able to do immeasurably more than we all ask or imagine, according to his power that is at work within us, to him be the glory in the church and in Christ Jesus throughout all generations, for ever and ever! Amen.'

[2] James Garlow, *The Covenant: A Study of God's Extraordinary Love for You*, Beacon Hill Press, Kansas City, MO, 1999.

[3] Pete Greig, *God on Mute: Engaging the Silence of Unanswered Prayer*, Kingsway Publications, Eastbourne, 2007.

Prayer Group Guide

- Most prayer groups focus on intercession. How will the teaching in this chapter shape your intercession?
- How does our discussion of 'meetings' affect your faith in the power of intercession?
- How is God seeking to use you to accomplish his purposes on the earth?
- In your particular situation, what will it mean to 'persist and persevere' in intercessory prayer?

CHAPTER 4
Spiritual warfare: how to wage war…on our knees

More Than a Metaphor?

SPIRITUAL warfare is more than a metaphor, but just what is a metaphor? According to dictionary.com it is: 'A figure of speech in which a term or phrase is applied to something to which it is not literally applicable in order to suggest a resemblance…'[4]

Numerous metaphors have been used to describe corporate Christian life. In the New Testament, the Church[5] is represented as: the flock, of which Jesus is the Shepherd (John 10:16); the body of Christ, of which Jesus is the head (Romans 12:5); a temple, of which Jesus is the cornerstone (1 Peter 2:4,5); a kingdom, over which Jesus is king (Colossians 1:12,13); a bride, for whom Jesus is the bridegroom (Ephesians 5:25-32). Salvationists, of course, are especially interested in the Bible's references to 'the army of God' (1 Chronicles 12:12). Is this expression a metaphor? Author Anthony Castle doesn't think so: 'If we are a metaphorical army in a metaphorical war', he writes, 'then we are not really an army and this is not a war.'[6]

The language of warfare permeates Scripture: Christians are 'soldiers' (Philippians 2:25; 2 Timothy 3:4; Philemon 1:2); they are engaged in a 'struggle' (Hebrews 12:4; Ephesians 6:12); they 'fight' (1 Timothy 1:18; 2 Timothy 4:7); they are engaged in 'war' (2 Corinthians 10:4; 1 Peter 2:11). God gives us armour (Ephesians chapter 6:10-20) and weapons (2 Corinthians 6:7; 10:4) with which to attack the strongholds of Satan, whose name means 'adversary' or 'enemy'.[7]

But it is not a war of guns, bullets, bombs, riots and physical destruction. It involves our soul – our way of life, our priorities and attitudes. We love to fight, but we fight with love. For example, in

Ephesians 6:12 (*NLT*) the apostle Paul says: 'For we are not fighting against flesh-and-blood enemies, but against evil rulers and authorities of the unseen world, against mighty powers in this dark world, and against evil spirits in the heavenly places.'

In its original language, the Bible's military overtones are even more striking than our English translations suggest. For example the Greek word *paganus* is used in the New Testament to refer to 'independents' – those who don't depend on Jesus. In most other contexts, however, this word refers to people not engaged in military service.[8] Jesus is often called *kurios*, a title for a military commander.[9] This is why Castle concludes: 'Scripture employs a detailed militant rhetoric that easily supersedes any alternative image in frequency, depth and spiritual application.'[10]

Military imagery is a big part of Scripture's portrayal of everyday spiritual life. It is also a big part of the broader Christian narrative, especially its apocalyptic finale. Castle writes: 'The spiritual realms are plagued with wars that define our faith and steer the fate of creation (Daniel 10:13; Ephesians 6:12; Revelation 12:7), until Jesus returns to "make war" against Satan and his nations' (Revelation chapter 19).[11]

Militant Christianity is expressed in various ways in God's church.[12] Not surprisingly, prayer is a focus of many of these movements.

Western Christians are beginning to grasp what their comrades in the developing world have long known – that we are engaged in a spiritual war with eternal consequences. Many images of Christian life are valid and enrich our understanding of the people of God. In these days of intense evil, God is mobilizing and deploying his army to fight the forces of evil and rescue souls from sin and hell!

Among the psalms most quoted in the New Testament are Psalms 2, 110 and 118 – all of them warfare prayers.[13] Why is this the case? Eugene Peterson explains: 'Massive engines of persecution and scorn were against them [the first apostles]. They had neither weapons nor votes. They had little money and no prestige. Why didn't they have mental breakdowns? Why didn't they cut and run? They prayed.'[14]

And when they prayed, they prayed warfare prayers.[15]

Is Ephesians 6:12 metaphorical? 'For our struggle is not against flesh and blood, but against the rulers, against the authorities, against the powers of this dark world and against the spiritual forces of evil in the heavenly realms.' It seems that Paul is introducing us to the literal reality, not the metaphor, of Christian life. We are engaged in a spiritual war. That makes prayer a high-stakes enterprise.

Paul is not alone: in Daniel's famous intercession, recorded in chapters nine and ten of the book of Daniel, we glimpse the supernatural battles occurring in response to prayer. Archangels and demons engage in real combat instigated by godly prayer.

What about Jesus' prayers? What do they teach us? Look at the verb tenses in the Lord's Prayer (Matthew 6:9-13):

- Our Father in Heaven, hallowed be your name (present).
- Your kingdom come, your will be done on earth as it is in Heaven (present).
- Give us today our daily bread (present).
- Forgive us our debts (present), as we also have forgiven our debtors.
- And lead us not into temptation, but deliver us from the evil one (present).

The Lord's Prayer addresses an ongoing struggle. God has empowered us to triumph in this struggle. Note the subject in the second clause of Matthew 18:18, 'I tell you the truth, whatever you bind on earth will be bound in heaven, and whatever you loose on earth will be loosed in heaven.' It is not God but we who are doing the binding and the loosing.

Two things to keep in mind when engaging in spiritual warfare:

1. Christianity is about community – 1 John 1:3.
2. You shouldn't go to war by yourself – Luke 10:1.

While you can pray effectively by yourself, Christianity is about community, and warfare prayers are most effective when they are corporate. Even when you are praying by yourself, it is helpful to pray in the plural, to pray for those who constitute your Christian community. It is unwise to live in spiritual isolation and it is unwise to fight in spiritual isolation. We don't advocate confronting the enemy alone when it is possible to confront him corporately. If you are in Christ, then you have the advantage no matter what the situation is – but even the apostles campaigned in groups.

Worship as Warfare

What is the first commandment? 'You shall have no other gods before me' (Exodus 20:3). Throughout the Scriptures this injunction is repeated: 'Love the Lord your God with all your heart, and with all your soul and with all your strength' (Deuteronomy 6:5; chapters 11, 13 and 22; Matthew 22:37; Mark 12:30; Luke 10:27).

Why is this principle important to spiritual warfare? Because God is a jealous god and he is our Commander in Chief. If our loyalties are divided, how can we hear the voice of the Lord of Hosts, the Lord Mighty in Battle? How can the Lord be confident in our trustworthiness unless our devotion to him is complete?

Every time God sent Moses to tell Pharaoh 'Let my people go', this instruction also included the phrase, '…so that they may worship me' (Exodus 7:16; 8:1; 8:20; 9:1; 9:13; 10:3). This represents the eternal truth, also contained in the new covenant, that we have been set free from bondage, delivered from enslaving sin in order to worship God and only God. When we worship God we are doing so as those set free from our tormentor. While this is not its primary purpose, in the context of warfare, worship of Yahweh by the redeemed mocks (Psalm 2:4-5 uses words like 'laughs', 'scoffs', 'rebukes', 'terrifies' – 'mocks' is a synonym) the one who comes to steal, kill and destroy. We are delivered!

As the people of God gather to worship God, they align themselves with God in opposition to Satan. We rejoice at the victory of God through Jesus Christ, not only in us, but also in the nations and for eternity, thereby demonstrating our freedom from worry, anxiety, intimidation and fear. Worship is an act of war!

'From the lips of children and infants you have ordained praise because of your enemies, to silence the foe and the avenger' (Psalm 8:2 *NIV 1984*).

Who's in Charge Here?

To whom does the world belong? The answer is three-fold.

1. '*The earth is the Lord's*, and everything in it, the world, and all who live in it' (Psalm 24:1 *NIV 1984*, our italics).

2. 'The highest heavens belong to the Lord, but the earth he has given to mankind' (Psalm 115:16 *NIV 1984*).

3. 'I will not say much more to you, for the *prince of this world* is coming. He has no hold over me' (John 14:30 *NIV 2010*, our italics). [Three times in John's Gospel Jesus refers to Satan as 'the prince of this world' – see John 12:31; 16:11.]

From the beginning, the Lord gave authority and responsibility on the earth to humans. However, our first parents, Adam and Eve, forfeited that authority by their disobedience and so Satan became 'the prince of this world' – a form of authority, to be sure, but one negated by Jesus' sacrifice on the cross.

Humans forfeited their authority on the earth and a human had to regain that authority. That human was *the man Christ Jesus*. Christ's victory therefore gives those who remain in him tremendous authority in spiritual warfare. We speak, pray and live all in the name of the one who defeated sin, hell and the grave.

[4] http://dictionary.reference.com/browse/metaphor

[5] Greek: Ekklesia - assembly, 'that which is called out'.

[6] Anthony Castle, 'Are We a Metaphor?', *Journal of Aggressive Christianity*, 11, April-May 2006.

[7] Anthony Castle, ibid.

[8] Phil Needham, *Community in Mission: a Salvationist Ecclesiology*, 126, The Salvation Army, 1987.

[9] Phil Needham, ibid.

[10] Anthony Castle, ibid.

[11] Anthony Castle, ibid (the last four paragraphs have leaned on Castle's research).

[12] Militant Christian movements include The Cause, Extreme Prophetic, Generals of Intercession, The Spiritual Warfare Movement, The War Room, The Final Quest, the 24-7 Prayer Movement, the various Watchmen Ministries, The Jesus Army, Blood 'N Fire Ministries, The Salvation Army, and this book, with its accompanying website (www.armyonitsknees.org), and related initiatives.

[13] Sunder Krishnan, *The Conquest of Inner Space: Learning the Language of Prayer*, 129, Scarlet Cord Press, Toronto, 2003.

[14] Eugene Peterson, *Reversed Thunder: The Revelation of John and The Praying Imagination*, 87, HarperCollins, 1991.

[15] Sunder Krishnan, ibid, 130.

Prayer Group Guide

- What is your perspective on spiritual warfare?
- How do you participate in it as a praying community?
- How do you protect yourselves in spiritual warfare?
- How do you exercise God-given authority in prayer?

CHAPTER 5
Prayer and fasting: losing leads to finding

FASTING is a puzzle. It is a powerful spiritual discipline, yet Satan has warped our understanding of it so much that many Christians don't practise it. How did this happen? Like so many of the enemy's schemes, it began with a distortion of Scripture.

The Bible instructs us not to make a big deal of fasting. It is properly done so discreetly that others don't even know about it (Matthew 6:18). Satan has exaggerated this counsel into a command *never* to talk about fasting. As a result, even devout Christians hear so little about fasting that they assume it is irrelevant or obsolete.

In the same passage, Jesus tells us not to look sombre while fasting, 'as the hypocrites do' (Matthew 6:16). Most Christians rightly recoil as soon as they hear someone say 'hypocrite', so determined are they not to be associated with this ugly word. Unfortunately, Satan has used this impulse as a way to frighten people away from fasting, as though there were intrinsically a link between fasting and hypocrisy. A classic case of throwing out the baby with the bathwater!

In Matthew chapter 9, Jesus is asked why his disciples feast while the Pharisees fast. He replies that you don't fast while you're with the bridegroom for a pre-wedding celebration (Matthew 9:14-15). Satan distorts this teaching, too, causing many Christians to assume: 'Well, Jesus is still with us and he hasn't actually married "the bride" yet, so I guess fasting isn't necessary!' However, verse 15 states clearly that Jesus would be 'taken away' from the disciples, after which they would fast. If we forget verse 15, we remove a potent spiritual weapon from our arsenal and leave ourselves more vulnerable to temptation, especially that of indulgence (more on this below).

Some of the people seen fasting in the New Testament are not especially ordinary. There is Anna, a widow who lived for 84 years in the temple (Luke 2:37). In one of Jesus' parables, a Pharisee boasts of his fasting in a prayer and is essentially ignored by God (Luke 18:12). Then, in the book of Acts, Paul's enemies swear not to eat or drink until he has been killed (Acts 23:12). (Paul lived for many more years. Unsurprisingly, perhaps, we don't hear of these enemies again.) Are these the kinds of people who fast – recluses, Pharisees and conspirators? What about ordinary believers?

Of course, many giants of the Christian faith have also been devoted to fasting. Yet even their example has perversely been used to *dissuade* believers from fasting. There is the argument from modesty: 'Who am I to reach for such heights?' Or the argument from fear: 'What if it's too hard? What if striving to be better prompts a spiritual attack?' Too often, this kind of thinking leads Christians to settle for less than God intends for them – or, at the very least, to go to battle without all the weapons he makes available to us.

When we think of those who have fasted throughout church history, we sometimes call up images of crazed, masochistic zealots. We consign fasting to the 'insane extremist' file, along with self-flagellation, hair shirts, vows of silence and pillar hermits. Who wants to be a freak?

And so we don't fast as we should.

We asked *how* Satan deceives us in this way. It's also worth asking *why* he deceives us in this way. Our answer: fasting, when wielded by a godly warrior, is a supernaturally powerful weapon.

Jesus our Model

Jesus was and is truly and properly God. He is our Redeemer and our Saviour. But he is also our role model. Although he *is* truly and properly God, he is *also* truly and properly human. The signs and wonders he displayed, the purity he exhibited, the compassion and mercy he demonstrated – all of these are possible for us as well. 'As the Father has sent me,' Jesus said, 'I also send you' (John 20:21 *NASB*). He is the example for us to imitate – and not only imitate, but surpass:

'He who believes in me, the works that I do, he will do also; and greater works than these he will do' (John 14:12 *NASB*). How can this be? How can we do 'greater' things than Christ did? And what does it mean to be 'sent' by Jesus?

In *The Hidden Power of Prayer and Fasting*,[16] Mahesh Chavda likens our task to that of a gymnast. Just as gymnasts must master elementary moves, such as the forward roll, before they can master more advanced ones, so we must practise the 'first works' of Jesus before we can accomplish the 'greater' works he promised.

Consider how before commencing his public ministry Jesus went into the wilderness to fast for 40 days (Luke 4:1-2). He returned from the wilderness 'in the power of the Spirit' (4:14). It was thus after fasting that Jesus began ministering with 'authority and power' (4:36). If fasting was a key to Jesus' effectiveness, it must be so for his disciples. Fasting and prayer are the 'first works' we must perform if we want to do the greater works to which Christ calls us.

Authority vs. Power

The Gospel of Matthew tells us of the disciples' inability to free a boy from demonic torment. After driving out the demon himself, Jesus rebuked his disciples for their ineffectiveness (Matthew 17:14-21). He expected them to perform miracles; after all, he was the one who had given them the authority to do so: 'He called his twelve disciples to him and gave them authority to drive out evil spirits and to heal every disease and sickness' (Matthew 10:1 *NIV 1984*). However, only those who have been spiritually and physically disciplined through prayer and fasting can exercise such authority. As believers, we too will face challenges and confront evils that can only be overcome in this way. We therefore neglect the 'fasted life' to our own detriment.

The Purpose of Fasting

Today most societies in the West are prone to overeating. It might even be said of us what Paul said of the 'enemies of the cross of Christ. Their god is their stomach' (Philippians 3:18-19). In such a context, fasting is a radical practice. Through fasting we put the flesh in its place and the Holy Spirit in first place. We teach our bodies and our appetites patience. We affirm that we do not live by bread alone, but by every word that comes from the mouth of God. By fasting we declare that our hunger for God is greater than our hunger for our next meal.

God does not change. He will not be manipulated. Our fasting does not persuade him to do something against his will and it certainly doesn't impress him as a display of piety. *We* are the ones changed through fasting. The psalmist David wrote that he humbled himself with fasting (Psalm 35:13).

Fasting has often been one means of 'self-denial', including in early-day Salvation Army history when people were invited to go without 'pudding' or dessert (a type of fasting from sweets for a set period of time) in order to exercise self-denial and give to the poor. It is a voluntary practice whereby we lay down certain privileges, deny or delay appetites and so on. Short of physical death, fasting is one way to lay down or relinquish aspects of life such as food, comfort, appetites and indulgences (1 John 3:16).

When we are aware of someone in trouble, we can enter into fasting and prayer for them, setting aside our appetites and our physical comfort for the sake of that person. Fasting helps us redirect our energies toward God, toward the Scriptures and toward intercession. It is one way to deny yourself, take up your cross and follow Jesus (Matthew 16:24).

The Lord's Expectations

In the Old Testament, fasting is often a pre-requisite for revival. In the book of Joel, the people of God are challenged to 'declare a holy fast, call a sacred assembly' (2:15). God then promises: 'And afterward, I will pour out my Spirit on all people' (2:28). Is it possible that revival is delayed in our day, at least in part, as a result of our failure to fast? How often do we choose self-indulgence and fleshly satisfaction over self-denial and spiritual vitality?

In the Sermon on the Mount, Jesus taught his disciples how to pray and fast. It was his expectation that they would do both (Matthew 6:5, 16-

17). What should our expectation be? Remember Jesus' words: 'If anyone would come after me, he must deny himself' (Matthew 16:24).

Benefits of Fasting

Through fasting we humble ourselves. We know from the book of James that God gives grace and favour to the humble (4:10). At the same time, fasting gives us power over temptation. Just look at Jesus' example in Luke chapter 4.

In Acts we read of Christians corporately fasting and praying for a clearer understanding of God's will. What would happen if we fasted when approaching important decisions?

Which Fast?

There are many ways to fast. In the Bible, fasting usually means going without food or fluids for a definite period of time – anywhere from a day or two to well over a month. Some fasts are routine, others are extraordinary or 'occasional'. God may call you to refrain from something harmless simply in order to re-establish your priorities, or he may call you to abstain from harmful practices, such as gossip. This is also a kind of fast.

In *Fasting for Spiritual Breakthrough: A Guide to Nine Biblical Fasts*,[17] Elmer Towns catalogues the various fasts described in the Bible. These include: the 'Samuel fast', in which communities fast as a way of seeking the Lord's guidance (1 Samuel chapter 7) and the 'Ezra fast', in which they fast as a way of seeking his protection (Ezra 8:21-22). Individuals crying out to God in times of trouble may undertake the 'Elijah fast' (1 Kings 19:2-8). The 'Disciples' fast' is a way of developing the spiritual authority to heal and cast out demons (Matthew 17:21 *NASB* [this verse is not in all translations]). The 'Saint Paul fast' (Acts chapter 27) is for individual spiritual insight, while the 'Daniel fast' is for physical health and strength (Daniel 1:8-16). Finally, the 'Esther fast' is a communal fast for deliverance (Esther 4:16).

Pioneers of Prayer and Fasting

Queen Esther called her people to enter a corporate fast for their deliverance. John the Baptist, who prepared the way for Christ, lived perhaps the ultimate 'fasted lifestyle' (Mark 1:1-8). It was during a period of fasting that God spoke to Cornelius, a Roman centurion, about visiting Peter – an encounter that led to a pivotal new understanding of the gospel's universality (Acts 10:30-31). Paul fasted for protection during a fierce storm, Daniel fasted as a gesture of both personal and collective repentance (Daniel chapter 9) and Jesus began his public ministry immediately after a fast.

The church fathers Polycarp and Tertullian fasted. So did Martin Luther, John Calvin, John Knox and John Wesley. Wesley was so committed to fasting that he would not approve candidates for ministry who did not fast twice a week! How would that policy affect leader recruitment today? How would it affect our impact?

Whenever he felt that his spiritual strength was waning, Charles Finney would immediately enter a three-day fast. It is said that after a fast, Finney would be so filled with the Holy Spirit that people felt an overwhelming sense of conviction at the mere sight of him.

Jonathan Edwards and Charles Haddon Spurgeon, two of the greatest preachers of all time, fasted in order to be more effective in the pulpit. Surely a worthwhile investment!

'When You Fast...'

Which type of fast does God desire for you? Are you called to enter a short-term 'refreshing' fast, like Finney's, or a long-term season of fasting, such as the one many Christians undertake over the 40 days of Lent?

God may be calling you to a lifestyle of continuous abstention from something. Perhaps he wants you to give up or reduce your consumption of certain unhealthy foods. Perhaps you have leisure activities that are not in themselves harmful, but which sometimes take too high a priority in your life and from which you may need to 'fast' for a time. Fasting is one of the best ways to re-establish – in your spirit and in your habits – God as the foremost passion of your life. The Internet, television, telephones, sports, movies: no matter how innocuous it may seem, anything that crowds out God should cede way to him through fasting.

May God inspire us to enter into the 'first works' of Jesus and may the result be a surge of 'greater works' in our midst.

Fasting as a Call to Voluntary Weakness

Fasting embodies the paradoxes of God's kingdom. Look at its manifestations:

- Losing leads to finding (Matthew 10:39).
- Dying leads to living (2 Corinthians 4:11, Romans 4:25 and 5:10, 1 John 3:14).
- Giving leads to receiving (Luke 6:38, Colossians 3:22-24, Matthew 10:8).
- Humility leads to exaltation (James 4:10, 1 Peter 5:6).
- Weakness leads to strength (2 Corinthians 12:9).

Let's take the last verse as an example: 'My grace is sufficient for you, for my power is made perfect in weakness.'

The Lord said this directly to Paul. What was the context?

- Paul was struggling with a 'thorn in the flesh'. He speaks of a 'messenger of Satan' sent to torment him (2 Corinthians 12:7).
- He was beset by enemies at every turn, 'in danger in the city, in danger in the country, in danger at sea' (2 Corinthians 11:26).
- He was painfully conscious of his own weakness (2 Corinthians 11:28-29).

Paul's experience illustrates the old saying: 'Our extremity is God's opportunity' or, in the words of this song:

He giveth more grace as our burdens grow greater,
He sendeth more strength as our labours increase;
To added afflictions he addeth his mercy,
To multiplied trials he multiplies peace.

When we have exhausted our store of endurance,
When our strength has failed ere the day is half-done,

When we reach the end of our hoarded resources
Our Father's full giving is only begun.

His love has no limits, his grace has no measure,
His power no boundary known unto men;
For out of his infinite riches in Jesus
He giveth, and giveth, and giveth again.
Annie Johnson Flint *SASB* No 579

Fasting is about God's strength revealed in our weakness. It is about denying oneself for the glory of Christ – and for the benefit of others. Paul writes to his loved ones, 'I will very gladly spend and be spent for you' (2 Corinthians 12:15 *King James Version*).

This is a kingdom principle. Remember, however, that there are two kinds of weakness: involuntary and voluntary. Involuntary weakness arises from persecution, calamity and demonic attacks. Fasting is a form of voluntary weakness: its purpose is for God's power to be perfected in us.

'But he said to me, "My grace is sufficient for you, for my power is made perfect in weakness." Therefore I will boast all the more gladly about my weaknesses, so that Christ's power may rest on me. That is why, for Christ's sake, I delight in weaknesses, in insults, in hardships, in persecutions, in difficulties. For when I am weak, then I am strong' (2 Corinthians 12:9-10).

Discipline the Appetites, Nourish the Spirit

Why fast?

- Traditional fasting: physical nourishment is sacrificed for spiritual nourishment.
- Prayer: time is sacrificed for communion with God.
- Giving: resources are sacrificed for others.
- Silence: pride is sacrificed for spiritual attentiveness.

You are not your own; you were bought at a high price. Your body is the temple of the Holy Spirit. You belong to God. He wants your spirit fed as well as your body.

What are you doing to nourish your spirit? We often forget that when our physical appetites are not in sync with the Holy Spirit, our spiritual capacity is diminished. Some 'appetites' are sinful and should never be indulged, while others are wholesome. Even with wholesome appetites, however, we must be wary of overindulgence. 'For, as I have often told you before and now say again even with tears, many live as enemies of the cross of Christ. Their destiny is destruction, their god is their stomach, and their glory is in their shame. Their mind is on earthly things' (Philippians 3:18-19).

Even our basic appetite for food can be distorted. God intended eating as an enjoyable way to strengthen our bodies; it is a legitimate part of our celebration of God's goodness. Without discipline, however, food can quickly become an idol.

The misdirection of this legitimate appetite was an element in humanity's first sin: 'When the woman saw that the fruit of the tree was good for food and pleasing to the eye, and also desirable for gaining wisdom, she took some and ate it. She also gave some to her husband, who was with her, and he ate it' (Genesis 3:6).

The same problem appears elsewhere in Scripture, sometimes in surprising places. The 'sin of Sodom', for example, is conventionally understood to be homosexuality. Recently, however, scholars have noted that Sodom is punished in part because its inhabitants neglected 'the poor and needy'. One of the sins of Sodom, it would seem, was injustice. But in the same text, 'fullness of food' is also listed: 'Look, this was the iniquity of your sister Sodom: She and her daughter had pride, fullness of food, and abundance of idleness; neither did she strengthen the hand of the poor and needy (Ezekiel 16:49 *New King James Version*).

Our physical appetites are a source of strength, but they are harmful when allowed to stray outside of God's will. Our appetite for food can give rise to greed and gluttony. Our appetite for sex can give rise to fornication and abuse.

Consider the 'rich fool' Jesus describes in Luke chapter 12. His plan was to store up wealth for a life of ease – to 'take life easy; eat, drink and be merry' (v 19). God rebukes him as a 'fool' for putting his appetites before everything else.

In the desert, the Israelites similarly put their appetite for food and drink before everything else – even freedom.

'The rabble with them began to crave other food, and again the Israelites started wailing and said, "If only we had meat to eat! We remember the fish we ate in Egypt at no cost – also the cucumbers, melons, leeks, onions and garlic. But now we have lost our appetite; we never see anything but this manna!"' (Numbers 11:4-6).

The Psalmist tells us that God granted their desire, but at a steep cost: 'And he gave them their request; but sent leanness into their soul' (Psalm 106:15 *KJV*).

Your stomach is a false god and will leave you unsatisfied. Dethrone it…through fasting!

Synopsis of Scriptural Fasts

Why not try each of these seven fasts this year?

1. To avert calamity:
    - 1 Samuel 7:6
    - Jonah 3:3-5
    - Joel 1:14
2. To experience the power of God in personal ministry:
    - Jesus
    - Elijah (1 Kings 19)
    - Also worth considering are the examples of Martin Luther, John Wesley and Charles Finney.
3. Fasting for revival:
    - John the Baptist (Matthew 11:18)
    - Anna (Luke 2:37)
    - Apostle Paul (Acts 13:2-3)
    - Joel 1:14 and 2:15ff
    - Matthew 6:16-17

4. Fasting as an expression of sorrow or mourning:
    - David's sorrow (Psalm 69:10)
    - Saul and Jonathan (2 Samuel 1:12)
    - Abner (2 Samuel 3:35)
    - David's infant son (2 Samuel 12:16-23)
5. Fasting over the sin of a nation or city:
    - 1 Samuel 7:6
    - Nehemiah 9
    - Jonah 3:5
6. Preparation for a divine assignment:
    - Nehemiah 1:4
    - Ezra 8:21
    - Daniel 10:2-3
    - Acts 13:1-2
    - Acts 14:23
7. The 'bridegroom fast':

• 'Jesus answered, "How can the guests of the bridegroom mourn while he is with them? The time will come when the bridegroom will be taken from them; then they will fast"' (Matthew 9:15).

[16] Mahesh Chavda, *The Hidden Power of Prayer and Fasting*, Destiny Image, Shippensburg, PA, 1998.
[17] Elmer Towns, *Fasting for Spiritual Breakthrough: A Guide to Nine Biblical Fasts*, Regal Books Publications, Ventura, CA, 1996.

Prayer Group Guide

• How would routine fasting and prayer affect your lives, both individually and as a community of faith? How would it help you to become more like Christ?

• How much are you willing to sacrifice – what appetites are you willing to deny – in order to establish God's kingdom on the earth?

• Are you seeing 'greater works' in your community? What is the relationship between these works and the discipline of fasting?

CHAPTER 6
Rhythms of prayer: something for everyone

THIS chapter is a collection of prayers, poems, songs, stories and exercises to inspire you in prayer. Allow God to minister to your spirit as you enter the 'rhythm of prayer'!

Classic written prayers

Lorica of Saint Patrick *

(The Latin word *lorica* literally means 'body armour')

For my shield this day a mighty power:
The Holy Trinity!
Affirming threeness, confessing oneness,
In the making of all
Through Love…

For my shield this day I call:
Christ's power in his coming
And in his baptizing,
Christ's power in his dying
On the cross, his arising
From the tomb, his ascending;
Christ's power in his coming
For judgement and ending.

This day I call to me;
God's strength to direct me,

God's power to sustain me,
God's wisdom to guide me,
God's vision to light me,
God's ear to my hearing,
God's word to my speaking,
God's hand to uphold me,
God's pathway before me,
God's shield to protect me,
God's legions to save me,
From snares of the demons,
From evil enticements,
From failings of nature,
From one man or many
That seek to destroy me,
Anear or afar.

Around me I gather:
These forces to save
My soul and my body
From dark powers that assail me:
Against false prophesyings,
Against pagan devisings,
Against heretical lying
And false gods all around me.
Against spells cast by witches,
Against knowledge unlawful
That injures the body,
That injures the spirit.

By Christ this day my strong protector:
Christ beside me, Christ before me;
Christ behind me, Christ within me;
Christ beneath me, Christ above me;
Christ to the right of me, Christ to the left of me;

Christ in my lying, my sitting, my rising;
Christ in heart of all who meet me,
Christ on tongue of all who meet me,
Christ in eye of all who see me,
Christ in ear of all who hear me.

* Adapted from the numerous versions of this prayer available online.

Personal Confession of Sin

I come into your presence, heavenly Father, giving thanks for the great blessings that I constantly receive from you. I give you praise and meditate on your Word, asking the things that are necessary for life and salvation. In preparing myself to worship you, I kneel in silence and, with a repentant heart, I confess my sins, that I may receive forgiveness by your goodness and mercy. I confess my sins against you and others.

Merciful God, I confess that I have sinned against you in thought, word and deed, by what I have done, and by what I have left undone. I have not loved you with my whole heart; I have not loved my neighbour as myself. I am truly sorry and I humbly repent. In the name of Jesus Christ, have mercy on me and forgive me; that I may delight in your will and walk in your ways, to your glory. Amen.

Almighty God have mercy on me, forgive me all my sins through my Lord Jesus Christ, strengthen me in all goodness and by the power of the Holy Spirit keep me in eternal life.
Amen.

The Nicene Creed

We believe in one God the Father Almighty, Maker of Heaven and earth, and of all things visible and invisible.

And in one Lord Jesus Christ, the only-begotten Son of God, begotten of his Father before all worlds, God of God, Light of Light, very God of very God, begotten, not made, being of one substance with the Father by whom all things were made.

Who for us men and for our salvation came down from Heaven, and was incarnate by the Holy Ghost of the Virgin Mary, and was made man, and was crucified also for us under Pontius Pilate. He suffered and was buried, and the third day he rose again according to the Scriptures, and ascended into Heaven, and sitteth on the right hand of the Father. And he shall come again with glory to judge both the quick and the dead; whose kingdom shall have no end.

And we believe in the Holy Ghost, Lord and Giver of life, who proceedeth from the Father and the Son, who with the Father and the Son together is worshiped and glorified, who spake by the prophets.

And we believe in one holy catholic and apostolic Church. We acknowledge one baptism for the remission of sins. And we look for the resurrection of the dead, and the life of the world to come.

Prayer of a Minor Prophet

Lord Jesus, I come to thee for spiritual preparation. Lay thy hand upon me. Anoint me with the oil of the New Testament prophet. Forbid that I should become a religious scribe and thus lose my prophetic calling.

Save me from the curse that lies dark across the modern clergy, the curse of compromise, of imitation, of professionalism. Save me from the error of judging a church by its size, its popularity or the amount of its yearly offering.

Help me to remember that I am a prophet – not a promoter, not a religious manager, but a prophet. Let me never become a slave to crowds. Heal my soul of carnal ambitions and deliver me from the itch for publicity. Save me from bondage to things.

Let me not waste my days puttering around the house. Lay thy terror upon me, O God, and drive me to the place of prayer where I may wrestle with principalities and powers and the rulers of the darkness of this world.

Deliver me from overeating and late sleeping. Teach me self-discipline that I may be a good soldier of Jesus Christ.

A.W. Tozer

Army

When we were made
The sky was full
Of steeples and of spires,
With churches of a thousand kinds
To suit each man's desires.
And priests and pastors hurried
In their thousands to their task.
Why did You make this 'Army-Church',
Am I allowed to ask?
With bandsmen in the organ loft
And songsters in the choir,
And brilliant banners blazing
With the motto 'Blood and Fire'?

Was it because with incense
And the chanting of The Creed
You wanted Your own shock-troops
Of a very diff'rent breed!
And with the more sedate of saints
The rougher sort as well,
Irrev'rently to shake the living
Daylights out of Hell!!

General John Gowans
The War Cry, 16 July 1983, New York

Silence and solitude

You are going out to meet someone very important. You are meeting with the lover of your soul.

Make sure you are physically comfortable. For some this may mean walking around, for others it will mean remaining seated. Pay attention to your environment, but be still inwardly. Try to sense the presence of God both in and around you.

Scripture meditation: read Psalm 139 slowly and deliberately, as a prayer – a personal conversation between you and the Lord.

- Thank the Lord for his tender care for you. Be as detailed as possible. Cite specific evidence of God's care for you – what he's saved you from and what he's saved you for.
- Ask the Holy Spirit to bring to your remembrance an occasion in your childhood or youth when Jesus was present with you – perhaps one you'd forgotten, or one in which you only now recognize his presence. Allow the Holy Spirit to show you the goodness and mercy of the Lord that has been following you all the days of your life (Psalm 23:6).
- Ask the Lord to reveal to you what he treasures in you and the purpose for which he made you. Listen for his response. An inner impression, a verse of Scripture, or a picture may come to your mind. Meditate on these. Reflect on God's love for you.

Centering prayer

- Intentionally place yourself in the presence of God, in the centre of his love. Be aware of your own breathing, your own heartbeat. Say to God, 'I am here. I am with you.'
- Choose a simple word or phrase that expresses your desire for God. Let this word focus your attention.
- If your mind wanders, don't worry. Gently guide your thoughts back to the centre of God's presence with the word or phrase that expresses your desire for him. *Be with* Jesus. Listen. Be still.
- Imagine that God's river of life runs through you. In its depths

the river is calm, but on the surface there are choppy waters and debris. Your distracting thoughts are amidst the debris, floating on the current. Release them and let the river of God's life carry them away.

• As you meet with Jesus, acknowledge that there are distractions, but continually return to share the moment with Jesus through your word of prayer.

• Rest in the centre of God's love. Trust that the Holy Spirit, who dwells deep in your own spirit, connects you with the Lord.

• As you attend to the Lord, enjoy his presence. Allow him to enjoy you, his child. You are his beloved one. Think about the Lord's delight in you – consider Psalm 139:17-18, Psalm 8 and Zephaniah 3:17.

Praying the Bible

'Praying the Bible' has been practised by Christians throughout history. In the Middle Ages, Celtic monks were known to pray or sing through the entire book of Psalms each week.

Here is a definition[18] of the word 'meditate' as used in the Old Testament: to mutter, to have a deep tone, to growl (like a lion over its prey), to groan, to utter, to moan (like a dove), to mourn.

Words Have Power

How did God first create the world? He spoke it into existence.

God created and sustains all things by the power of his word. We are made in his image. Therefore, our words are similarly endowed with power – both for creation and for destruction.

In Romans 10:8-10, Paul declares: '"The word is near you; it is in your mouth and in your heart", that is, the message concerning faith that we proclaim: if you declare with your mouth, "Jesus is Lord," and believe in your heart that God raised him from the dead, you will be saved. For it is with your heart that you believe and are justified, and it is with your mouth that you profess your faith and are saved.'

Our very salvation rests in part on what we 'confess' – on our spoken words. God has vested tremendous power in us: the power to go from death to life by our own words!

'The tongue has the power of life and death, and those who love it will eat its fruit' (Proverbs 18:21).

Words have power. You can use them to speak life or to speak death. That's why Satan specializes in prompting us to use our words for gossip, slander, bitterness, resentment, envy, cursing and other destructive purposes. As we read in James 3:9-11: 'With the tongue we praise our Lord and Father, and with it we curse human beings, who have been made in God's likeness. Out of the same mouth come praise and cursing. My brothers and sisters, this should not be. Can both fresh water and salt water flow from the same spring?'

Consistency in speaking life is one important manifestation of holiness.

How can we harness the power of words in prayer? One of the best ways we know of is *praying the Bible.*

Pray the Bible

Learn the language of the Spirit in order to express what is in your heart. Begin to pray actual Bible verses and chapters phrase by phrase, slowly and repetitively. The idea is to learn God's own thoughts and God's own vocabulary from Scripture.

Pray Out Loud

A classic verse on this subject is Joshua 1:8: 'Do not let this Book of the Law depart from your mouth; meditate on it day and night.'

Recall the Old Testament conception of 'meditate': to murmur, to mutter, to have a deep tone, to growl (like a lion over its prey), to groan, to utter, to moan (like a dove), to mourn.

Evidently the idea is to involve the vocal chords in some way, whether by growling, moaning, or muttering. So when you meditate on God's word, use your voice!

Here are two further reasons to pray out loud:

1. So you know when you have stopped!

2. Because it's hard to think about something else while *you're* talking! (See *Praying the Bible* by Wesley and Stacey Campbell.[19])

It was Ezekiel's practice to pray out loud: 'So I prophesied as I was commanded' (Ezekiel 37:7), or to put it another way: 'So I spoke these words just as he told me'.

Remember God's promise from Joel, recounted by Peter in Acts 2:17-18: 'In the last days, God says, I will pour out my Spirit on all people. Your sons and daughters will prophesy, your young men will see visions, your old men will dream dreams. Even on my servants, both men and women, I will pour out my Spirit in those days, and they will prophesy.'

And here is Jesus' teaching:

'This, then, is how you should pray:
"Our Father in Heaven,
hallowed be your name,
your kingdom come, your will be done
on earth as it is in Heaven."'
(Matthew 6:9-10)

A psalm of praise:

- Psalm 103

Meditate on Christ – his sacrifice and suffering:

- Isaiah 53
- Psalm 22
- Philippians 2

Meditate on Christ – the risen, glorified one:

- Revelation chapters 1, 4 and 5
- Colossians 1

Apostolic prayers for the church:

- Colossians 1
- Ephesians chapters 1 and 3

Rest confidently in union with Christ – the place with Christ in prayer where no words need to be said, no petitions requested, not even praise. Just silent communion with the Holy Spirit in Jesus Christ:

- Song of Songs 8:6-7

Praying The Salvation Army Song Book

- Songs of praise – 'Jesus Shall Conquer' No 173, 'Jesus the Name' No 60
- Songs of intercession – 'I am Praying' No 584
- Songs of holiness – 'Take Time to be Holy' No 458
- Songs of faith – 'Greater Things' No 769

Lectio Divina

Lectio Divina is Latin for 'sacred reading'.

Four steps:

1. *Lectio*: a selection or reading.
2. *Meditatio*: meditating or contemplating.
3. *Oratio*: speaking or praying.
4. *Contemplatio*: contemplation.

Here is another way to explain the same process:

1. Restful reading.
2. Mull it over.
3. Conversation and affinity.
4. Listen for the whisper – be still.

A suggested discipline:

1. *Lectio*: 10 minutes.
2. *Meditatio*: five minutes.
3. *Oratio*: 10 minutes.
4. *Contemplatio*: five minutes.

Thomas Aquinas: ways we read the Bible:

- **Literal**: the most direct, basic meaning of the words.

Luke 10:25-37: Jesus tells a story about a man who was beaten by robbers but helped by a man from a despised foreign country, Samaria.

- **Spiritual**: the theological meaning of the words.
- **Allegorical**: the figurative meaning of the words.

Jesus wants us to see that our 'neighbour' isn't just the person who lives next to us; we are all God's children and so we are all 'neighbours' in a spiritual sense.

- **Moral**: the meaning that inspires us to imitate Christ.

Jesus wants us to be like the Samaritan and help those in need, no matter who they are or where they are from.

- **Anagogical**: the mystical, largely hidden meaning of the words, often pointing at some aspect of the world to come.

The Kingdom of Heaven is a place of perfect healing, a place where earthly identities no longer matter.

Prayer walking

'Prayer walking' is a way of saturating a particular place and a particular community with prayer. This discipline draws our immediate, local concerns into the wider circle of God's loving attention. Such prayers are intercessory rather than devotional.

Scriptural support for prayer walking is found in Joshua 1:2-4, Psalm 2:8 and Luke 24:13.

How to prayer walk:

- You can prayer walk alone, but many people find that their prayers are more focused when expressed in the company of a friend.
- Pray audibly for clarity and agreement.
- Invite the spirit of God to accompany you, guiding your steps and your words.
- Be attentive during moments of silence. Allow the Holy Spirit to help you see with his eyes and pray with his heart.

• Address God directly when contending with darkness. Ask God to redeem people as he restrains the enemy.

• Read Scripture aloud. God breathed it and loves to bless it.

• Express God's thoughts in your own words.

Listening prayer

'My sheep listen to my voice; I know them, and they follow me' (John 10:27).

Preparation:

• Time.

• Supplies (Bible, pen, journal, water).

• Prayer (to hear from God and *not* to hear from the evil one).

• Location (a place free of distractions, a beautiful place, a sacred place).

Listening skills:

• Don't talk or think; be in a listening position.

• Allow God to interrupt your normal stream of thoughts.

Write:

• A question.

• A passage of Scripture.

• God's words to you.

Test:

• Is this word in accordance with God's character?

• Is it in accordance with Scripture?

• Seek affirmation and confirmation from godly people, or from evidence of God's work in your circumstances.

Circles of influence: a creative template for prayer

Lieut-Colonel Richard Munn

God seems to work in certain discernable and recognisable patterns – from the stunning cadence of the seasons to the remarkable biological similarities in his creatures. The rhythm of the seasons is beautifully reliable and the amazing likenesses to be found in the diversity of animal life – skeletal structure, digestive system, senses, and so on – imply that our Creator has a recognisable artistic style that, like a template, he can tweak. Yes, our God is lord of the aesthetic stencil and order.

This also appears to be so in the meta-narrative of Scripture. For instance, he seems to delight in revealing his power in the motif of death and resurrection – the Valley of Dry Bones, Lazarus and supremely in Jesus. He communicates his essence in light – the opening act of Creation, his guidance in the wilderness and, most sharply in Jesus, the Light of the World.

One of these divine patterns appears to be expanding circles. The overall sweep through Scripture moves from the solitary family of Abraham, Isaac and Jacob to the people of Israel to all people of the world. Jesus also applies the pattern working with a centrifugal force from the inner circle of Peter, James and John to the central 12 disciples to the greater 72 disciples (Luke 10).

I believe this can provide you and me with a pattern for prayer.

Not that long ago the Lord worked on me for several successive months with beautiful and forceful grace, calling me to become more creative and more disciplined in prayer. One of these outcomes was a template for prayer – Circles of Influence. It is precious to me and may be catalytic for you.

While the mould is objective, the pattern is yours – intensely so. If you're even moderately intrigued, complete the following inventory and see how the final silhouette emerges.

Let's start smack-dab in the middle.

Personal Prayers

You have a personal relationship with God so it's a natural place to pivot. This is central to the whole pattern. Even Jesus starts the expanding circle of his classic High Priestly Prayer (John 17) with prayers for himself.

- What does God continually seem to be revealing to you?
- What grace energizes you?
- What injustice grieves you?
- What passages of Scripture resonate with you?
- What divine insight has stirred you recently?
- What are the deep, immovable desires of your heart?

There is value to repetition, so form these responses into a sacred mantra. For instance, God once gave me a simple – yet powerful – prayer: 'Increase my capacity to love.' I say that many times a day; it does me good.

Prayers for Family

You have a primary area of influence with your family. It is likely that you have a more naturally intense bond of love and conviction with this group of people than any other.

It is here that we can start to use an important principle to add bold brush strokes to your pattern – the concept of authority. In Matthew 8 Jesus remarks on the muscular faith of the Roman centurion, who stuns Jesus with this perceptive observation: 'Just say the word, and my servant will be healed. For I myself am a man under authority, with soldiers under me. I tell this one, "Go," and he goes; and that one, "Come," and he comes. I say to my servant, "Do this," and he does it' (Matthew 8:8, 9).

A helpful way of phrasing this in prayer might be, 'By the authority given to me under Christ I extend my faith on behalf of…'

You have unusual and singular authority as a family-member to bring your kin to the throne of Christ. This is yours to be used. It is a sacred trust and should not be ignored or discarded or treated casually. My delight is to pray protective prayers for my wife and children; and prayers of honour for my parents:

- Name your spouse – call her blessed (Proverbs 31:28); call him righteous (Psalm 112).
- Name your children – Deuteronomy 6.

- Name your parents – The Ten Commandments.
- Name your siblings.
- Name your in-laws.
- Name your nieces and nephews.
- Name your cousins.
- Name your patchwork family.

Wow! I suspect you have quite a list.

Prayers for Leaders

You and I may have authority, but you know we are also under authority. 'You're gonna have to serve somebody' sang Bob Dylan, with sharp insight. So, it does us good to bless those who shoulder leadership and, of course, it will likely grace them. Besides that, the gospel injunction is to pray for our leaders.

Naming our leaders in prayer is a gift of respect and support, it keeps us humble, is a reminder that our leaders are human and is a balm during times of testing and disagreement:

- Who are your leaders?
- Who do you serve under?
    - o Political and national
    - o Denominational and church
    - o Employment
    - o Mentors

Prayers for Colleagues

We also have influence with people right alongside us, those we likely interact with many times in any given week. Such prayers can almost be quasi-clandestine; camouflaged agents of grace. Here we tap into the principles of mutuality and synergy. We energize the graces of unity and harmony. Romans 12 provides a good couple of sacred contours: 'In honour preferring one another' (v10) and 'Not thinking of ourselves more highly than we ought' (v3). Hmm…those two phrases alone add bracing dimensions:

- Name your work colleagues.
- Name your corps colleagues.
- Name your ideological colleagues.

Prayers for Friends

Phileo love is a rich biblical principle. Jesus himself remarkably says 'I have called you friends' (John 15:15) and John powerfully taps into the concept where he repeatedly writes 'Dear friends…' (1 John 4:1,7,11).

Our friends are God's gift to us; they mediate his love. Candidly, those of us who find comfort in our self-constructed portable walls should probably be especially grateful that we are 'befriended.'

Name your friends.

Prayers for Areas of Ministry Influence

You probably have an area of designated influence, even authority, in ministry. It is likely a formal assignment. This is yours to exert with great care, humility and confidence. For instance, if you are a youth worker, nobody can quite pray with more zeal, knowledge and insight for those kids than you. If you are a music group leader, you know the members of that ensemble like nobody else and can pray for their effectiveness and well-being with unusual clarity. The same goes for every group of which you are a part – in fact, for all of us in ministry.

You were likely given that sacred task in a rite-of-passage, before a community of faith. As a consequence you have immense capacity for influence in prayer; second to none, sacred authority in ministry. Please, do not leave this authority lying about for any competing entity to pick up, because pick it up they will. Consider:

- What are your specific ministry assignments?
- Name your community of faith.
- Who is in your small group?
- What councils, teams, boards or committees are you on?

Prayers for geographic regions

You and I are inhabitants of a simultaneously dark and beautiful world and that can mean a global influence in prayer. Jesus said it – we would be his witnesses 'to the ends of the earth' (Acts 1:8).

Certain regions, cities and towns are undoubtedly especially near and dear to us. We have inherent passion and 'authority' as a consequence. Try these as markers:

- Name your turf – the land of your birth, the rock from which you are cut.
- Outline your geographic life history – your 'boundary lines' (Psalm 16).
- What are your 'special places' – neighbourhood, city or region?
- Where are your supernatural burdens and/or passion?
- Do you have any specific callings? e.g. a country wracked with conflict?
- Name the regions that break your heart.

Final thoughts – craft your own style here, your imprint or logo, so-to-speak, on this rippling template. Here are mine:

- I pray for young leaders – the Timothys who will one day lead us.
- I love to pray for those I have had the privilege to lead to Christ.
- I pray for the appointments where we have served over the years.
- I pray for ministry assignments before us.

This is a continually evolving assignment – it is never truly completed. This gives extra vibrancy to such praying. Sometimes the Lord will even give release from certain assignments, a 'mission accomplished' seal.

[18] www.blueletterbible.org/lang/lexicon/lexicon.cfm?Strongs=H1897&t=KJV

[19] Wesley and Stacey Campbell, *Praying The Bible*, Regal Books/Gospel Light, Ventura, CA, 2002.

CHAPTER 7
The spiritual disciplines: improve with practice

RECENTLY my son Zion and I [Stephen] were memorising 2 Timothy 1:7: 'For God did not give us a spirit of timidity, but a spirit of power, of love and of self-discipline.' When we got to the last word, Zion looked worried. To him, 'discipline' suggested punishment and brought to mind the stern faces of disappointed parents and teachers.

As is standard practice in our family during moments of hermeneutical confusion, I responded with a detailed etymology found at www.etymonline.com:

> early 13c., "penitential chastisement; punishment", from O.Fr. *descepline* (11c.) "discipline, physical punishment; teaching; suffering; martyrdom", and directly from L. *disciplina* "instruction given, teaching, learning, knowledge", also "object of instruction, knowledge, science, military discipline", from *discipulus* (see *disciple*). Sense of "treatment that corrects or punishes" is from notion of "order necessary for instruction". The Latin word is glossed in O.E. by *þeodscipe*. Meaning "branch of instruction or education" is first recorded late 14c. Meaning "military training" is from late 15c; that of "orderly conduct as a result of training" is from c.1500.

Or something like that.

Even if you only skimmed or (as is more likely) entirely skipped the previous paragraph, you'll know that the word 'discipline' connotes toughness, rigour and difficulty. For many, including my son, it also has overtones of correction or rebuke. It's usually not a pleasant thought.

Attach the mysterious and intangible concept of 'spirit', as in 'a spirit of self-discipline', and we shouldn't be surprised to find that the result is often overlooked.

Overlooked, but indispensable.

Remember 'WWJD?' ('What would Jesus do?')? Here's a somewhat less bracelet-friendly follow-up question: 'Can I do what Jesus did?' If we can't answer 'yes' to this question, then 'WWJD?' will elicit only frustration and puzzlement. So if we *can* do what Jesus did, *how* do we do it?

No Excuses

We *can* do what Jesus did – and even greater things. Hallelujah! Consider these Scriptures:

> 'God did not give us a spirit of timidity, but a spirit of power, of love and of self-discipline' (2 Timothy 1:7).
>
> 'His divine power has given us everything we need for life and godliness through our knowledge of him' (2 Peter 1:3).
>
> 'God is faithful; he will not let you be tempted beyond what you can bear. But when you are tempted, he will also provide a way out so that you can stand up under it' (1 Corinthians 10:13).
>
> 'Being confident of this, that he who began a good work in you will carry it on to completion until the day of Christ Jesus' (Philippians 1:6).
>
> 'May God himself...sanctify you through and through. May your whole spirit, soul and body be kept blameless at the coming of our Lord Jesus Christ. The one who calls you is faithful and he will do it' (1 Thessalonians 5:23-24).

Spiritual Disciplines

With these promises in mind, we should view spiritual disciplines as habits that help propel us toward God and transform us more fully into the likeness of Jesus Christ.

In Richard Foster's *Celebration of Discipline: The Path to Spiritual Growth*[20] the author mentions two broad categories of spiritual disciplines:

1. Abstinence.
2. Engagement.

1. Disciplines of Abstinence

Disciplines of abstinence counteract tendencies toward sins of commission. They are informed by Peter's instruction to 'abstain from sinful desires, which wage war against your soul' (1 Peter 2:11).

Disciplines of abstinence:

- Fasting.
- Solitude.
- Silence.
- Chastity.
- Frugality.
- Secrecy.
- Simplicity.

We devoted Chapter 5 to fasting (partly because it has been especially neglected). Now let's look at what some great Christian writers have to say about the other disciplines of abstinence.

Solitude

The Quaker William Penn wrote the following in his *Some Fruits of Solitude in Reflection and Maxims*:[21]

> 'We understand little of the Works of God, either in Nature or Grace. We pursue False Knowledge, and Mistake Education extremely. We are violent in our Affections, Confused and Immethodical in our whole Life; making That a Burden, which was given for a Blessing; and so of little Comfort to ourselves or others; Misapprehending the true Notion of Happiness, and so missing of the Right Use of Life, and Way of happy Living.
>
> 'And till we are persuaded to stop, and step a little aside, out of the noisy Crowd and Incumbering Hurry of the World, and Calmly take a Prospect of Things, it will be impossible we should be able to make a right Judgement of ourselves or know our own Misery. But

after we have made the just Reckonings which Retirement will help us to, we shall begin to think the World in great measure Mad, and that we have been in a sort of Bedlam all this while.'

[The capitalisation of the source text has been retained, but some words have been updated for modern usage – e.g. 'burthen' is now 'burden'.]

Silence

Saint Teresa of Ávila devotes a large portion of her book *The Way of Perfection*[22] to the 'Prayer of Quiet'. Quaker pioneer John Woolman testifies, in his *Journal*,[23] to his experience of the value of silence:

'One day, being under a strong exercise of spirit, I stood up and said some words in a meeting; but not keeping close to the divine opening, I said more than was required of me. Being soon sensible of my error, I was afflicted in mind some weeks, without any light or comfort, even to that degree that I could not take satisfaction in anything. I remembered God, and was troubled, and in the depth of my distress he had pity upon me, and sent the Comforter. I then felt forgiveness for my offence; my mind became calm and quiet, and I was truly thankful to my gracious Redeemer for his mercies. About six weeks after this, feeling the spring of divine love opened and a concern to speak, I said a few words in a meeting, in which I found peace. Being thus humbled and disciplined under the cross, my understanding became more strengthened to distinguish the pure Spirit which inwardly moves upon the heart, and which taught me to wait in silence sometimes many weeks together, until I felt that rise which prepares the creature to stand like a trumpet, through which the Lord speaks to his flock.'

Chastity

In *The Rules and Exercises of Holy Living* (1650),[24] the English clergyman Jeremy Taylor writes:

'Chastity is that duty which was mystically intended by God in the law of circumcision. It is the circumcision of the heart, the cutting off all superfluity of naughtiness, and a suppression of all irregular desires in the matters of sensual or carnal pleasure...Chastity is that grace which forbids and restrains all these, keeping the body and soul pure in that state in which it is placed by God, whether of the single or of the married life; concerning which our duty is thus described by Saint Paul: "For this is the will of God, even your sanctification, that ye should abstain from fornication: that every one of you should know how to possess his vessel in sanctification and honour, not in the lust of concupiscence, even as the Gentiles which know not God" (1 Thessalonians 4:3-5).

'Chastity is either abstinence or continence. Abstinence is that of virgins or widows; continence of married persons.'

Frugality

John Wesley, in his *Journal*,[25] writes:

'I gave our brethren a solemn caution not to 'love the world, neither the things of the world'. This will be their grand danger: as they are industrious and frugal, they must needs increase in goods.'

John Calvin, in his *Commentary on Daniel*,[26] offers this prayer on frugality:

'Grant, Almighty God, as long as our pilgrimage in this world continues, that we may feed on such diet for the necessities of the flesh as may never corrupt us; and may we never be led aside from sobriety, but may we learn to use our abundance by preferring abstinence in the midst of plenty. Grant also, that we may patiently endure want and famine, and eat and drink with such liberty as always to set before us the glory of thy name. Lastly, may our very frugality lead us to aspire after that fullness by which we shall be completely refreshed, when the glory of thy countenance shall appear to us in Heaven, through Jesus Christ our Lord. Amen.'

Secrecy

The 18th century Catholic theologian Francois de Fénelon writes:

> 'We are very severe about externals, and do not look within. While we are scrupulous about a superficial display of virtue, we do not regard the coldness of our secret hearts towards God. We fear him more than we love him…
>
> 'How unspeakable are the blessings that piety bestows; pure, disinterested piety, piety that never fails, that does good in secret!'

Simplicity

In the original 'self-examination' used by Methodists, the first question concerned simplicity: 'Have I been simple and recollected in everything I said or did? Have I (a) been simple in everything, that is, looked upon God, my Good, my Pattern, my one Desire, my Disposer, Parent of Good; acted wholly for Him; bounded my views with the present action or hour? (b) Recollected? That is, has this simple view been distinct and uninterrupted?'

Wesley, the founder of the Methodist movement, preached on 'simplicity of heart':

> 'We are then simple of heart when the eye of our mind is fixed singly on God; when in all things we aim at God alone, as our portion, our happiness, our strength, our exceeding great reward; our all, in time and eternity. This is simplicity; when a steady view, a single intention of promoting his glory, of doing and suffering his blessed will, runs through our whole soul, fills all our heart, and is the constant spring of all our thoughts, desires, and purposes.'

Taylor offers instructions for maintaining simplicity:

> 'Accustom thyself to cut off all superfluity in the provisions of thy life, for our desires will enlarge beyond the present possession so long as all the things of this world are unsatisfying: if, therefore, you suffer them to extend beyond the measures of necessity or moderated conveniency, they will still swell: but you reduce them

to a little compass when you make nature to be your limit. We must more take care that our desires should cease than that they should be satisfied: and, therefore, reducing them in narrow scantlings and small proportions is the best instrument to redeem their trouble…'

2. Disciplines of Engagement

The disciplines of engagement counteract our tendency toward sins of omission. They include:

- Study
- Worship
- Celebration
- Service
- Prayer
- Fellowship
- Submission
- Confession

Again, let's consider each of these disciplines individually.

Study

In the preface to his *Notes on the Whole Bible – Old Testament* (1765),[27] Wesley writes:

'If you desire to read the Scripture in such a manner as may most effectually answer this end, would it not be advisable:

1. To set apart a little time, if you can, every morning and evening for that purpose?

2. At each time if you have leisure, to read a chapter out of the Old, and one out of the New Testament: if you cannot do this, to take a single chapter, or a part of one?

3. To read this with a single eye, to know the whole will of God, and a fixt [sic] resolution to do it? In order to know his will, you should,

4. Have a constant eye to the analogy of faith; the connexion and harmony there is between those grand,

> fundamental doctrines, original sin, justification by faith, the new birth, inward and outward holiness.
>
> 5. Serious and earnest prayer should be constantly used, before we consult the oracles of God, seeing 'Scripture can only be understood thro' the same Spirit whereby it was given'. Our reading should likewise be closed with prayer, that what we read may be written on our hearts.
>
> 6. It might also be of use, if while we read, we were frequently to pause, and examine ourselves by what we read, both with regard to our hearts, and lives. This would furnish us with matter of praise, where we found God had enabled us to conform to his blessed will, and matter of humiliation and prayer, where we were conscious of having fallen short. And whatever light you then receive, should be used to the uttermost, and that immediately. Let there be no delay. Whatever you resolve, begin to execute the first moment you can. So shall you find this word to be indeed the power of God unto present and eternal salvation.'

Worship

'By the pathway of duty flows the river of God's grace' – so goes Sidney Cox's well-known chorus. In other words, when we are disciplined and intentional in our worship, we avail ourselves of God's grace. As Dallas Willard says in *The Spirit of the Disciplines: Understanding How God Changes Lives*,[28] 'The direct divine encounter is not essential to true worship, and it may also occur outside of the context of purposeful worship…Worship is our part, even though divinely assisted, and therefore it can be a discipline for the spiritual life.'

Willard cites the 13th century bishop Albertus Magnus, who writes that we 'find God through God himself; that is, we pass by the Manhood into the Godhood, by the wounds of humanity into the depths of his divinity'.

Celebration

How should we engage in the discipline of celebration? Moses' sister Miriam led the Hebrews in victorious dancing after their exodus, and David famously became 'undignified' in celebratory worship. In *The Christian's Secret of a Happy Life*,[29] Hannah Whitall Smith portrays the celebrating heart:

> 'You will spring out to meet his dear will with an eager joy. Even his slightest wish will become a binding law to you, which it would fairly break your heart to disobey. You will glory in the very narrowness of the path he marks out for you, and will pity with an infinite pity the poor far-off ones who have missed this precious joy. The obligations of love will be to you its sweetest privileges; and the right you have acquired to lavish the uttermost abandonment of all that you have upon your Lord, will seem to lift you into a region of unspeakable glory. The perfect happiness of perfect obedience will dawn upon your soul, and you will begin to know something of what Jesus meant when he said, "I delight to do thy will, O my God."'

Willard reviews the basics of the discipline of celebration:

> 'We engage in celebration when we enjoy ourselves, our life, our world, in conjunction with our faith and confidence in God's greatness, beauty, and goodness. We concentrate on our life and world as God's work and as God's gift to us.'

Service

Taylor links service to love:

> 'Love is as communicative as fire, as busy and as active, and it hath four twin-daughters, extreme like each other; and but that the doctors of the school have done, as Thamar's midwife did, who bound a scarlet thread, something to distinguish them, it would be very hard to call them asunder. Their names are, 1. Mercy; 2. Beneficence or well-doing; 3. Liberality; and, 4. Alms; which, by a special privilege, hath obtained to be called Charity…The first and

> the last only are duties of Christianity. The second and third are circumstances and adjuncts of these duties; for liberality increases the degree of alms, making our gift greater; and beneficence extends it to more persons and orders of men, spreading it wider. The former makes us sometimes to give more than need by the necessity of beggars, and serves the needs and conveniences of persons and supplies circumstances; whereas properly alms are doles and largesses to the necessities of nature, and giving remedies to their miseries.'

We will never run out of ways to express our love through service, Taylor writes, because 'the works of mercy are so many as the affections of mercy have objects, or as the world hath kinds of misery.'

Prayer

If you're reading this book, it's likely that you already have some interest in prayer. It's also likely that you know what prayer involves – and that it's a lot more than most people think. Methodist theologian John Fletcher writes that in prayer:

> 'You strive, pray, resist, but are the little better; yet, pray, strive, resist on. It is good to be tried and to get a blessing in the very fire. We shall then know how to value it properly. Do you pray, strive, resist against wanderings with any steadiness and do you do it in cheerful hope to overcome through the blood of the Lamb? When you have been unhinged from Christ in mind or heart, do you, with stronger indignation against wanderings, a calmer expectation of the assistance of the Spirit and a deeper agony of faith, seek to be avenged of your adversary? Do you imitate the importunate widow?'

In his *Memoirs*,[30] David Brainerd gives us a glimpse of his own devotion to prayer – a devotion that explains his great effectiveness as a missionary:

> 'In the evening, though tired, was enabled to continue instant in prayer for some time. Spent the time in reading, meditation and

prayer, til the evening was far spent: was grieved to think that I could not watch unto prayer the whole night. But blessèd be God, Heaven is a place of continual and incessant devotion.'

Fellowship

'We proclaim to you what we have seen and heard, so that you also may have fellowship with us. And our fellowship is with the Father and with his Son, Jesus Christ' (1 John 1:3).

Christian fellowship means more than a cup of coffee after church on a Sunday morning. As salvation warriors, our fellowship is in the fight. Such fellowship is only possible when we are first in fellowship with God. Christian fellowship arises when God pervades our lives. This is a kind of spiritual discipline. It is also essential to growth in Christ. As Willard observes, 'Personalities united can contain more of God and sustain the force of his greater presence much better than scattered individuals.'

Submission

Thomas à Kempis, in his timeless classic *The Imitation of Christ*,[31] explores the idea of submission:

> 'It is a very great thing to obey, to live under a superior and not to be one's own master, for it is much safer to be subject than it is to command. Many live in obedience more from necessity than from love. Such become discontented and dejected on the slightest pretext; they will never gain peace of mind unless they subject themselves wholeheartedly for the love of God.
>
> 'Go where you may, you will find no rest except in humble obedience to the rule of authority. Dreams of happiness expected from change and different places have deceived many.
>
> 'Everyone, it is true, wishes to do as he pleases and is attracted to those who agree with him. But if God be among us, we must at times give up our opinions for the blessings of peace.
>
> 'Furthermore, who is so wise that he can have full knowledge of everything? Do not trust too much in your own opinions, but be

willing to listen to those of others. If, though your own be good, you accept another's opinion for love of God, you will gain much more merit; for I have often heard that it is safer to listen to advice and take it than to give it. It may happen, too, that while one's own opinion may be good, refusal to agree with others when reason and occasion demand it, is a sign of pride and obstinacy.'

Christian submission means not just submission to God, but to each other. According to Willard, 'The war of Jesus knows no submission outside of the context of mutual submission of all to all' (Ephesians 5:21; Philippians 2:3).

Confession

In *Life Together*,[32] Dietrich Bonhoeffer writes:

'A man who confesses his sins in the presence of a brother knows that he is no longer alone with himself; he experiences the presence of God in the reality of the other person. As long as I am by myself in the confession of my sins everything remains in the dark; but in the presence of a brother the sin has to be brought into the light.'

Bonhoeffer quotes Martin Luther's *Great Catechism*: 'When I admonish men to come to confession, I am simply urging them to be Christians.'

We hope this brief primer on the spiritual disciplines has been edifying and inspiring. The sources we've quoted here are well worth investigating further – both the centuries-old writings and more recent ones such as Willard's *The Spirit of the Disciplines* or Richard Foster's *Celebration of Discipline*.

Practising the spiritual disciplines allows the river of God's grace to flow through our lives. They are a means of abstaining from worldly temptations, engaging with God and further promoting his glory and good purposes.

[20] Richard Foster, *Celebration of Discipline: The Path to Spiritual Growth*, Hodder & Stoughton, 2008.
[21] Edmund Gosse and William Penn, *Some Fruits of Solitude in Reflection and Maxims*, Kessinger Publishing, Whitefish, MT, 2010.
[22] Saint Teresa of Ávila, *The Way of Perfection*, Cosimo Inc, New York, NY, 2007.
[23] John Woolman, *Journal*, www.strecorsoc.org/jwoolman/title.html
[24] Jeremy Taylor, *The Rules and Exercises of Holy Living*, http://www.ccel.org/ccel/taylor/holy_living.iv.iii.i.html
[25] John Wesley, *Journal*, www.ccel.org/ccel/wesley/journal.vi.xiii.iv.html
[26] John Calvin, *Commentary on Daniel*, www.ccel.org/ccel/calvin/calcom24.vii.ix.html
[27] John Wesley, *Notes on the Whole Bible – Old Testament*, http://www.ccel.org/ccel/wesley/notes.ii.i.html
[28] Dallas Willard, *The Spirit of the Disciplines: Understanding How God Changes Lives (Audiobook)*, Hodder & Stoughton, 1996.
[29] Hannah Whitall Smith, *The Christian's Secret of a Happy Life*, Whitaker House Books, New Kensington, PA, 1983.
[30] David Brainerd, *Memoirs*, Baker Books, Baker Publishing Group, Ada, MI, 1989.
[31] Thomas à Kempis, *The Imitation of Christ*, www.ccel.org/ccel/kempis/imitation.ONE.9.html
[32] Dietrich Bonhoeffer, *Life Together*, SCM Press, 1954.

Prayer Group Guide

• Try practising each of the spiritual disciplines. Keep a journal of the experience. How have these disciplines affected your daily life, especially your relationship with God?

• Consider practising the spiritual disciplines as a group. Make a record of the spiritual growth you experience together and keep it in your prayer room to inspire others.

CHAPTER 8

Non-stop prayer: it's happening in our day!

24-7 Prayer

THERE are many rhythms of prayer, and non-stop prayer – in which members of a Christian community take turns seeking God in uninterrupted succession – is among the most effective. In 1999 God stirred up two non-stop prayer movements, the International House of Prayer, based in Kansas City, USA, and the 24-7 Prayer Movement, which started in Chichester, England.

What began as a single month of non-stop prayer in Chichester's Revelation Church continued for several more, the prayer rosters filled with willing volunteers, until eventually the programme expanded into an ongoing global movement. The history of this movement, which continues to transform lives around the world, has been documented in a book, *Red Moon Rising*.[33]

The 24-7 movement was explicitly intended to 'turn the tide in youth culture'. The movement's website declares: 'The Body of Christ is blessing young people. But while the churches shrink, greed, injustice and spiritual hunger increase. Something has to change.'

The leaders of the 24-7 prayer movement identify similar movements throughout church history:

- Isaiah 62:6 – Isaiah calls upon the watchmen who will guard Jerusalem in prayer and instructs them *'never be silent day or night'*. This tradition of unceasing prayer is reiterated in the New Testament, both in the disciples' anticipation of Pentecost and in Paul's instruction to pray 'on all occasions' (Ephesians 6:18).
- Acts 1:14 – this tells us that the apostles 'all joined together constantly in prayer.'

• The Celtic Monks – unceasing prayer and petition is an important part of medieval church history. At Northern Ireland's Bangor Abbey, there were monks praying continually between AD559 and 759. In the 15th century, the Pope decreed that there should be continual prayer in a number of locations around the world.

• The Moravians – in the 18th century a small community of Moravian Christians, led by Count Nikolaus von Zinzendorf, began a prayer watch that would carry on, spanning generations, for more than 100 years. During these years this small movement sent in excess of 3,000 missionaries throughout Europe. They would reach most parts of the continent and counted among their converts the Wesley brothers, whose own movement shaped the young William Booth. Perpetual prayer is part of The Salvation Army's heritage!

A Test Case

The Salvation Army has been a major participant in today's global 24-7 prayer movement; there have now been years of ongoing Salvationist prayer in several countries.

Its participation in this movement officially began in the UK at the *Roots* conference in 2001, during which 1,500 people spent time in the prayer room. In the course of the following year 200 Salvation Army communities undertook similar extraordinary prayer commitments. From there, the movement spread – and continues to spread. Major Judith Bennett's 2009 book *White Cloud Soaring*[34] recounts the inspiring history of The Salvation Army's non-stop prayer efforts in New Zealand. Prayer brings revival! During the first year of non-stop prayer in The Salvation Army's USA Eastern Territory, Salvationists created more than 220 'prayer rooms'. This explosive increase in prayer is ushering in a new season of God's saving work in this region.

As of 2009, there are 18 Salvation Army training colleges linked in '24.7.5' prayer ('5' referring to The Salvation Army's five global 'zones').

Global Call to 24-7 Prayer – A Day and Night Cry for Justice

Prayer Reflections

'Picture God's people united in prayer, where one hour isn't enough in the prayer room and there is a desire for more, where children and youth are crying out for justice. Picture people committing themselves for a day, month, year or more of non-stop prayer and intentionally giving voice to the issues that are on their hearts. Picture faith increasing and prayers being answered. The good news is this beautiful imagery is happening in The Salvation Army. It is a reality.'[35]

Since 1 January 2011, Salvation Army territories, commands and regions have been praying as part of the *Global Call to 24-7 Prayer – A Day and Night Cry for Justice.*

The call comes from the parable of the persistent widow in Luke 18:7-8, where Jesus said: 'And will not God bring about justice for his chosen ones, who cry out to him day and night? I tell you, he will see that they get justice, and quickly.'

Hundreds of non-stop prayer rooms have housed extravagant prayer in 2011, including some that have been praying non-stop the whole year. The purpose of the Global Call is to motivate and focus attention on prayer throughout The Salvation Army's international family, with a united purpose in intercession – the need for justice for the oppressed.

Another aspect of the Global Call is the integration of prayer, justice and the arts. Crying out for deliverance from oppression through songs is part of Scripture and the history of the Church. This is why the website www.saytunes.com is supporting the Global Call to 24-7 Prayer through a Songs of Justice section on its website, to which Salvationist composers are contributing monthly.

An artistic project, Just Arts, is underway and will be linked to the 24-7 Prayer website and through this Salvationists worldwide can contribute and have access to music compositions, paintings, photographs, poems and other forms of creative writing related to prayer and justice. Latest resources and news are updated daily on the Global Call to 24-7 Prayer Facebook (facebook.com/saglobal247) and Twitter (@saglobal247) pages.

A renewal of prayer is happening in our day. We are called to be part of it.

In The Salvation Army, 24-7 prayer continues to expand. How will this movement develop in the years to come?

- Salvationists will still be praying – intentionally and intensively!
- Prayer rooms will be utilized by people of all ages, by soldiers, officers, friends and visitors, by those who come to us for help, by faithful local officers and by our divisional, territorial and international leaders.
- Prayer rooms will be established as a fixture of hundreds of Salvation Army communities and facilities. As a result, we will hear countless stories of people coming to know the love of Christ. There will be stories of healing – physical, emotional and spiritual – and of reconciliation.
- Fresh, creative ministries will arise from the time we commit to prayer. Flowing out of prayer rooms will be effective new ways of reaching out to the poor, the lost and the broken-hearted. Children at risk; oppressed, exploited women and hopeless men will find new hope in Christ.
- There will be an increase in outreach. Everyone who enters our places of worship will encounter revitalized Salvationists, hearts aflame with the love of God and attuned to the needs of others –

hearts that bear the evidence of continual communion with the Holy Spirit.

- Every Salvationist will be intent on growth in Christ through Bible study, group prayer, communal accountability and cooperative spiritual formation. There will be a desire to establish through discipleship what has been ignited through prayer.
- Everywhere, The Salvation Army will continue advancing – on its knees!

And where does it go from there? Only God knows!

[33] Pete Greig and Dave Roberts, *Red Moon Rising*, Kingsway Publications, 2004.
[34] Judith Bennett, *White Cloud Soaring*, Flag Publications, The Salvation Army, 2009.
[35] Based on Janet Munn's article 'Prayer Reflections', July-September, *All The World*, IHQ, 2011.

Prayer Group Guide

• Why not try practising the rhythms of prayer we have described and recording the results in your journal? Better yet, why not share those results with your praying community?

• It might be helpful to keep a communal prayer journal in your prayer room, so that intercessors can encourage and edify one another. Prayer is meant to be shared!

CHAPTER 9

The place where God dwells: a house of prayer for all nations

A Home for our Homeless God[36]

IT IS one of the great ironies of the Christian story – a homeless God. Strange as this idea may seem, it expresses an important aspect of God's relationship with humanity. This is not only because God identifies with the poor and marginalized, but also because we are all spiritually homeless until we find our home in Christ.

So why does a book on prayer talk about homelessness – God's and ours? We do this to shift our discussion from the realm of theory to that of relationships. Consider these simple questions:

- Where is God's home?
- What do you call 'home'?
- How far will God go to make his home with us?
- How far will we go to become God's home?
- What part does prayer play in enabling God to live in us?
- How big is God's house?

God announced that his house, the place where he dwells, would be a house of prayer. We must be that house.

A Place with God: Eden and the Patriarchs

At the 24-7 Prayer Conference held in Southampton, United Kingdom (UK) in September 2008, Pete Greig, one of the pioneers of 24-7 prayer, said that the strangest thing about the Bible is God's desire to be with humans.

Consider Isaiah 56:7: 'All these I will bring to my holy mountain and make them joyful in my house of prayer. Their burnt offerings and their sacrifices will be accepted on my altar; for my house will be called a house of prayer for all peoples' (*AB*).

Note that God's house is 'for all peoples', or all nations. You may recall that all three Synoptic gospels quote Jesus' reference to this passage (Matthew 21:13; Mark 11:17; Luke 19:46), suggesting that the theme of God's house was an important part of his message.

This makes sense, for as we consider the Bible's overarching story, we see that it is a story of God's longing to make himself at home with humanity, from the creation account in Genesis to John's declaration in Revelation 21:3, 'God's dwelling place is now among the people, and he will dwell with them.'

Where is God's home? In Psalm 24:1 we read, 'The earth is the Lord's and the fullness thereof; the world, and they that dwell therein' (*KJV*). Does this mean that God is at home on the earth? One way to answer this question is to look at God's relationship to the earth at creation, 'in the beginning'.

Eden

Even as God prepared the earth as a perfect dwelling place for humanity, he also anticipated enjoying communion with Adam and Eve on the earth. Genesis tells of the Lord 'walking in the garden in the cool of the day', implying that he was looking for Adam and Eve, hoping to fellowship with them. There was no need for a tabernacle or temple, a particular location for God, because the whole earth was his dwelling place, along with humankind.

God created a home for humans on the earth and invited them to make themselves at home there, where he, too, would be at home with them.

In Eden, God made his dwelling with Adam and Eve. Later, God made his dwelling with the Patriarchs, with the Hebrew people (in the Tabernacle, in the wilderness and in the Temple in Jerusalem), in Jesus Christ[37] and, from the day of Pentecost, in the people of God, the Church – the temple of the living God.

God the initiator – we the responders
God the pursuer – we the pursued
God the creator – we the created
God the provider – we the recipients
God the one who seeks – we the sought

The Ministry of Hospitality

When people visit your home, what preparations do you make? You probably clean the house and prepare a special meal. Especially dedicated hosts will even cater to their guests' unique tastes. Either way, preparing for guests takes work.

If we look through the opening chapters of Genesis, we find God in a stir of activity. Throughout chapter one we see that God 'created', 'said', 'saw', 'separated' and 'made'. In fact, action language is used in 26 of its 31 verses.

These verbs are all indicators of God acting as host, busily making arrangements for the arrival of humans, his special guests, his companions, the objects of his unique, devoted love. God was getting ready because company was coming!

But Why?

In Revelation 4:11 we read: 'Thou art worthy, O Lord, to receive glory and honour and power: for thou hast created all things, and *for thy pleasure* they are and were created' (our italics, *KJV*). Other translations render 'for thy pleasure' as 'by your will' or 'because you wanted it'. In other words, God created us not out of obligation, but out of joy.

Similarly, Isaiah 43:7 has God addressing 'everyone who is called by my name, *whom I created for my glory*, whom I formed and made' (our italics). The word for 'glory' used here is translated elsewhere as 'weight, honour, esteem, majesty, abundance, wealth'. Jesus says in Matthew 6:21, 'Where your treasure is there will your heart be also' (*KJV*). So if we are God's treasure, then his heart is with us. Imagine that! It turns on its head the regular perspective on our relationship with God. He treasures you! He created you; he planned each day you'll live; he thinks and thinks and thinks about you (Psalm 139); he went to ultimate ends to reconcile you to himself; he gives you every good and perfect gift.

In Psalm 8 humans are compared with *elohim*, a word that can be translated as 'angels', 'heavenly beings', or even God himself. Psalm 8:5 says that God has made humans 'a little lower than the angels' [*elohim*].

In summary, we were created from and for God's pleasure and glory and are of great worth to him. God's heart is in the same place as his treasure – with us. We were made a little lower than God himself, in his image and likeness, and are intended to commune with him.

We're programmed to:

- Have an open line of communication with him
- Hear the whisper of his voice
- Sense the prompting of his Spirit
- Enjoy the expressions of his love
- Bask in the warmth and security of his shadow
- Appreciate his approbation
- Thrive in his blessing
- Hide in his shelter and refuge
- Embrace his ways
- Imitate his works
- Live his life
- Have his mind
- Perfect holiness in reverence of him
- See what he's doing and do what we're seeing.

After the fall

However, despite the intimate relationship between God and (man) humans, Adam and Eve disobeyed him. 'So the Lord God banished him from the Garden of Eden to work the ground from which he had been taken. After he drove the man out, he placed on the east side of the Garden of Eden cherubim and a flaming sword flashing back and forth to guard the way to the tree of life' (Genesis 3:23-24).

What happened after the fall – to Adam and Eve, and to God? God drove Adam and Eve out of the Garden of Eden, out of fellowship with himself. Not only were Adam and Eve expelled from the home God had carefully prepared for them – God himself lost the 'home' he had shared with them. Through their rebellion, Adam and Eve had rejected God's hospitality, his offer to share a home with them on planet earth. Both God and humans lost a home on that day.

Walking with God

Let's contrast the conditions in which Adam and Eve 'walked with God' with those of Noah (Genesis 6:1-9).

In Eden we find God walking with humans in ideal conditions – paradise, literally. Yet Adam and Eve end up hiding from God, not walking with him: 'Then the man and his wife heard the sound of the Lord God as he was walking in the garden in the cool of the day, and they hid from the Lord God among the trees of the garden' (Genesis 3:8).

Read Genesis 6:1-9. Note the contrast with chapters one and two. From heaven on earth to hell on earth – wickedness and perversion everywhere, with Noah the sole exception. Yet even in those circumstances Noah walked with God and led a blameless life.

During a trip to Greece I [Janet] visited the island of Patmos – the place where, it is traditionally held, the exiled Apostle John wrote the book of Revelation. Pagan temples were plainly visible from the cave described in Revelation chapter 1. On the hilltops various sacrifices and other rituals would have been taking place in view of the place where John received his vision. I had previously imagined John on an isolated desert island, making it easier for him to receive a vision from God than for me or anyone else subject to the distractions of contemporary Western culture. My visit to Patmos ruined that excuse.

How much do our circumstances affect our ability to walk with God – to get on our knees? When we consider the conditions faced by Noah and John, can we still blame our surroundings for any shallowness in our walk with God? Of the examples we have considered so far, the only ones recorded as blaming others were Adam and Eve – and they were living in paradise.

'I said, "Fill the Earth!"'

God's instruction to Noah and his family was what it had been to Adam and Eve: 'Then God blessed Noah and his sons, saying to them, "Be fruitful and increase in number and fill the earth"' (Genesis 9:1). But by Genesis chapter 11 look at what is happening: 'Come, let us build ourselves a city, with a tower that reaches to the heavens, so that we may make a name for ourselves; otherwise we will be scattered over the face of the whole earth' (Genesis 11:4).

The people who were instructed to spread throughout the whole earth at the LORD's direction were already wanting to settle, to build and to make a name for themselves. In Isaiah 43:7 we are told that God's people are called by his name, but at Babel the people wanted to make a name for themselves by reaching up to heaven.

The Patriarchs

Read Genesis 12:1-4. The covenant outlined in Genesis chapter 12 between God and Abram is described by Paul in Galatians 3:8 as 'the gospel in advance'. Since the fall, God has required a covenant before abiding with humans. In other words, covenant precedes cohabitation:

- Genesis 3:21 (bloodshed).
- Genesis 6:18-22; 9:1-17 (a promise, a sign, a commitment; the commitment from Noah, too, in response involved 'all life on earth').
- Genesis 12:1; 22:1-19 (Abram's call/covenant).

As we consider the example of Abram and Isaac we are led to ask: 'How far will God go to dwell with humanity?'

'Abraham answered, "God himself will provide the lamb for the burnt offering, my son"' (Genesis 22:8).

God's dwelling on the earth has moved from the whole earth (Psalm 24:1) to Abraham and his family, which would become a nation.

In Genesis 12, God calls Abram to leave his home and family and country but promises to bless every home and family and country through his obedience. What is God after? Our relentless God, our jealous God, unwilling to be deterred from being in relationship with humankind, despite having been rejected by Adam and Eve, chose a people, a family, who became a nation, and the first family contact was Abram. God was again looking to establish a dwelling with humans.

The Lord asks Abram to leave his home in order to start a special family with whom God would dwell. Eventually, God would reaffirm his desire to dwell not only with Abram's family, but also with all families and all nations.

A Mobile Home: the Tabernacle

Many years later God again reveals his desires when he meets with Moses on Mount Sinai.

He wants to bring his people out of Egypt, out of exile and back into relationship with himself. He has heard their cries and is responsive to them. He intends to set the Hebrews free from slavery and dwell with them. 'The Israelites groaned in their slavery and cried out, and their cry for help…went up to God. God heard their groaning and he remembered his covenant with Abraham, with Isaac and with Jacob' (Exodus 2:23-24).

The Lord then gave thorough instructions to Moses to create a dwelling for himself among the people – such was his longing to be among his people. It takes five full chapters in the Bible (Exodus 25-30) to describe it!

What is the significance of the elaborately detailed instructions the Lord gives to Moses concerning the Tabernacle? Among other things, it is clear that he is deeply interested in and committed to establishing himself among the people. The Tabernacle was to be in the midst of the Hebrew people, even while they remained in the wilderness. The Tabernacle stood in the middle of the camp and the Ark of the Covenant, representing the presence of God, was in the centre of the Tabernacle. The Ark of the Covenant is the first item God describes as he instructs Moses on setting up the Tabernacle, establishing his intention to be present in the middle of the Tabernacle,[38] in the middle of the Hebrew camp – even in the middle of the wilderness.

Why is the Tabernacle portable? Because God moves with his people. He is not static and will not be left behind. By his presence in a mobile Tabernacle the Lord communicates that he intends to travel with his people, to remain among them as they carry the reality of his presence to all nations. Years later, David set his heart on building the Temple. He wanted to please God by constructing a place for God to dwell. How does God respond? Although welcoming the idea and blessing David's desire, he promises the honour of building the Temple to David's son, Solomon.

God will not be outdone! When David is inspired to create a dwelling place for God – the Temple in Jerusalem – God says, 'You want to build a house for me? David, I'm going to make *your* house great, an everlasting house, from which salvation will come!' When it comes to homemaking, no one outdoes God. He commits himself to the house of David forever – such is his determination to dwell with humans.

This determination was earlier demonstrated in God's devotion to the Hebrew midwives who defied Pharaoh's murderous decree in order to preserve life, including the life of baby Moses. 'Because the midwives feared God, he established households for them' (see Exodus 1:20-21 *NASB* and 2 Samuel 7:12ff). Exodus 25:8-9 reads: 'Then have them make a *sanctuary* for me, and I will dwell among them. Make this *Tabernacle* and all its furnishings exactly like the pattern I will show you' (our italics).

The word translated 'sanctuary' is *miqdash*, meaning a consecrated, holy place. The word translated 'tabernacle' is *mishkan*, which can mean a residence, a shepherd's hut, an animal's lair, or even the grave. *Mishkan* occurs 139 times in the Hebrew Bible while *miqdash* occurs 74 times.

Note the contrast between these two words and how often the preferred word is the one referring to an 'ordinary' dwelling. In fact, there are more verses of the Pentateuch devoted to the Tabernacle, or *mishkan*, than any other object.

The following verses help us understand the importance of the Tabernacle:

- Exodus 25:22: 'There, above the cover between the two cherubim that are over the Ark of the Covenant law, *I will meet with you* and give you all my commands for the Israelites' (our italics).
- Exodus 29:42-43: 'For the generations to come this burnt offering is to be made regularly at the entrance to the tent of meeting, before the Lord. There *I will meet you* and speak to you; there also *I will meet with the Israelites*, and the place will be consecrated by my glory' (our italics).
- Exodus 30:6: 'Put the altar in front of the curtain that shields the Ark of the Covenant law – before the atonement cover that is over the tablets of the covenant law – where *I will meet with you*' (our italics).
- Exodus 30:36: 'Grind some of it to powder and place it in front of the Ark of the Covenant law in the tent of meeting, where *I will meet with you*. It shall be most holy to you' (our italics).

Tabernacle: the place where God meets with his people. This place is an ordinary residence.

The New Testament echoes this concept when Paul writes of the presence of the Holy Spirit dwelling inside the believer: 'But we have this treasure in jars of clay to show that this all-surpassing power is from God and not from us' (2 Corinthians 4:7).

I [Janet] heard a three year-old boy crying for his father's attention. The father said, 'Use your words, Jed'. The boy responded simply, 'Daddy, I want to be with you!' Who could resist? Similarly, the Lord, the king of the universe, in incomprehensible humility says to us: 'I want to be with you.'

Meeting with God

In the Old Testament, the word we translate 'meet' means 'appoint, fix a place or time, betroth, give in marriage, meet by agreement, come together'.

This same word is used in Exodus 21:8-9 to refer to betrothal and again in Exodus 25:22 and 29:42-43 to denote God meeting with humans in the Tabernacle.

On the cross a bridegroom and his bride were reunited – a meeting similar to that which took place between my fiancé and me, as described earlier on page 24.

Ephesians 5:25-27 reads: 'Husbands, love your wives, just as Christ loved the church and gave himself up for her to make her holy, cleansing her by the washing with water through the word, and to present her to himself as a radiant church, without stain or wrinkle or any other blemish, but holy and blameless'.

God says, 'I will meet with you. You can meet with me.' Through Jesus' sacrifice God created a *meeting* between God and humans.

Psalm 85:10 reads: 'Love and faithfulness *meet* together; righteousness and peace kiss each other' (our italics).

2 Corinthians 5:18 reads: 'All this is from God, who reconciled us to himself through Christ and gave us the *ministry of reconciliation*' (our italics).

The Tabernacle was a place of atonement for sin. Important meetings took place in that 'ordinary' dwelling place. Through our *meeting* with God in prayer others are able to meet with God. This is true intercession: meeting with God in order to arrange a meeting between God and others. It is a ministry of reconciliation.

The Bible devotes only two chapters to the creation of the world, but 50 chapters to the construction of the Tabernacle. Why this surprising imbalance? Perhaps because while God didn't need instructions to make a home for humans, humans did need instructions to make a home for God.

In the detailed list of the elements and contents of the Tabernacle outlined in Exodus chapters 25-30, the first item listed is the Ark of the Covenant – in other words, the presence of God with his people. In Hebrews 8:5 we are told that the Tabernacle is 'a copy and shadow of what is in Heaven'. Heaven is the reality upon which the Tabernacle is modelled, like a sketch. This is reinforced in Revelation 15:5 as well: 'After this I looked, and I saw in Heaven the Temple – that is, the Tabernacle of the covenant law…'

Look at this example from the New Testament in Luke 24:25-27, 44-45. As Jesus is walking along the road to Emmaus following his resurrection, he explains to his disciples the symbolism and prophetic significance of the Old Testament Scriptures: how these things *had to happen*, had to be fulfilled – and were fulfilled in him.

When the Hebrew people were in the wilderness they were surrounded by reminders of the presence of God in the midst of their camp – the Tabernacle, the Ark of the Covenant and the pillars of fire and cloud.

Eventually, however, God became fed up with them because, despite all the miracles, provision, deliverance and manifestations he had given them, the Hebrews stubbornly rebelled against him.

In Exodus 33:3 he says, terrifyingly: '*But I will not go with you*, because you are a stiff-necked people and I might destroy you on the way' (our italics). It's as if God is saying, 'I am so holy that if I am with you when you rebel you would be utterly destroyed. I cannot dwell with you when you are like this' (see v 5). Therefore he removes his presence.

In the Bible we catch glimpses of the all-knowing God in the act of making a decision. In the book of Exodus he allows a human being, Moses, to influence a decision regarding his presence. Exodus 33:15-16 records Moses saying to God, 'If your presence does not go with us, do not send us up from here…What else will distinguish me and your people from all the other people on the face of the earth?'

In verse 17 God replies, 'I will do the very thing you have asked, because I am pleased with you and I know you by name.' Let's learn from Moses and this conversation in Exodus chapter 33. Let's ask boldly and persistently of God. Let's believe that the Lord responds to our cries, hears our voice and answers. Ask!

Like the father of the prodigal son written about in Luke 15, God the Father yearns to welcome his children home. He longs to dwell again with his people, to make his presence obvious among them.

In The Salvation Army we have a song, the chorus of which invites the lost to come home to God:

Come home, come home!
Ye who are weary, come home!

Earnestly, tenderly, Jesus is calling,
Calling, O sinner, come home!
Will Lamartine Thompson *SASB* No 264

But we can also invite the Lord to come and be at home with his people:

Come home, come home!
You who are worthy, come home!
Earnestly, tenderly, Lord, we are calling,
Calling, O Saviour, come home!

God in the Neighbourhood: the Incarnation

To help us understand God's relationship with us, let's retrace the steps of his pursuit of humans – what we might see as 'The Incredible Shrinking Home of God':

- God's dwelling place is the whole earth at creation – an all-encompassing home.
- After humanity's rebellion, God establishes his dwelling within a much smaller scope – a people, a family, a nation, beginning with Abram.
- A home smaller than a nation: the Tabernacle in the wilderness then the Temple in Jerusalem – God dwelling in one place, establishing his presence within a fixed structure.
- Finally, rejected and rebelled against, God says: 'I will dwell among them myself, as one of them' – that is, in the flesh of one man, the Lord Jesus Christ.

Jesus fulfils and embodies all eight elements of the Tabernacle (see Exodus chapter 35):

1. *Door* (v 17 and John 10:9) 'I am the door. If anyone enters by me, he will be saved, and will go in and out and find pasture' (*NKJV*).
2. *Bread of the Presence* (v 13 and John 6:35) 'Then Jesus declared, "I am the bread of life. Whoever comes to me will

never go hungry, and whoever believes in me will never be thirsty."'

3. *Altar of Incense* (v 15 and Hebrews 7:25) 'Therefore he is able to save completely those who come to God through him, because he always lives to intercede for them.'

4. *Mercy Seat* (v 12, Leviticus 16:14-15 and Romans 3:25) 'God presented Christ as a sacrifice of atonement, through the shedding of his blood – to be received by faith. He did this to demonstrate his righteousness, because in his forbearance he had left the sins committed beforehand unpunished.'

5. *Basin* (v 16 and John 13:8) 'Jesus answered, "Unless I wash you, you have no part with me."'

6. *Lampstand* (v 14 and John 8:12) 'When Jesus spoke again to the people, he said, "I am the light of the world. Whoever follows me will never walk in darkness, but will have the light of life."'

7. *Veil* (v 12 and Hebrews 10:19-21) 'Therefore, brothers and sisters, since we have confidence to enter the Most Holy Place by the blood of Jesus, by a new and living way opened for us through the curtain, that is, his body, and since we have a great priest over the house of God…'

8. *Tabernacle* (John 1:14) 'The Word became flesh and made his dwelling among us. We have seen his glory, the glory of the one and only Son, who came from the Father, full of grace and truth.'

Jesus explicitly describes himself as a 'temple' in John 2:18-19: 'The Jews were upset. They asked, "What credentials can you present to justify this?" Jesus answered, "Tear down this Temple and in three days I'll put it back together"' (*TM*).

Jesus implies that he symbolizes everything that the Temple symbolized and offers everything that the Temple offered to the people of God. And yet he is not limited physically as the Temple building was. Jesus represents our rightful dwelling place (note the theme of our being 'in Christ', referenced 93 times in the New Testament).

Moved into the Neighbourhood: Tabernacled among Us

Compare Genesis 1:1-5 with John 1:1-5: Jewish rabbis would have understood the use of 'in the beginning' as an allusion to the creation account in Genesis, with the 'Word' equated with the Creator.

We see the Tabernacle arrangements in Exodus 25:8-9: 'Then have them make a sanctuary for me, and I will dwell among them. Make this Tabernacle and all its furnishings exactly like the pattern I will show you.'

Hebrews 8:5 suggests that these prior things from Exodus were patterns or moulds: 'They serve at a sanctuary that is a copy and shadow of what is in heaven. This is why Moses was warned when he was about to build the Tabernacle: "See to it that you make everything according to the pattern shown you on the mountain"'.

We read in Luke 24:27: 'And beginning with Moses and all the Prophets, he explained to them what was said in all the Scriptures concerning himself.' This tells us that these things had to happen, must happen and that they are about Jesus himself.

Compare Exodus 25:8-9 with John 1:14. *Shakan* (to dwell) always assumes a surrounding community or neighbourhood (tabernacle) – God is a God of relationship. This 'tabernacling' is not just God dwelling on the earth – not just God-in-the-flesh – but God with us, God in the neighbourhood. From the beginning God intended to be with us on the earth.

Truly and Properly Human

In the first century church there was a heresy known as 'Docetism'. Its error concerned the nature of Christ. Docetic teaching held that Jesus' body was only an appearance – that is, he *seemed* incarnate in the flesh (the Greek word *dokeo* means 'to seem'), but wasn't really human. Therefore, the message of John 1:1,14 – 'In the beginning was the Word, and the Word was with God, and the Word was God... the Word became flesh, and dwelt among us…' – was intolerable for the Docetics.

The Apostle John refutes Docetic teaching in his epistles. For example, in 1 John 4:2-3 (*NASB*) he writes, 'By this you know the Spirit of God: every spirit that confesses that Jesus Christ has come in the flesh is from God; and every spirit that does not confess Jesus is not from God; this is the spirit of the antichrist, of which you have heard that it is coming, and now it is already in the world.' Also 'For many deceivers have gone out into the world, those who do not acknowledge Jesus Christ as coming in the flesh. This is the deceiver and the antichrist' (2 John v 7 *NASB*).

And – in agreement with John – The Salvation Army's fourth doctrine states: 'We believe that in the person of Jesus Christ the Divine and human natures are united, so that he is truly and properly God and truly and properly man.'

Truly and Properly God

Read these New Testament passages that speak of Jesus' divinity:

- John 1:1-5: Rabbis would have understood this to refer to Yahweh the creator.
- Colossians 1:15-20: He is before all things; in him all things hold together. All things were created by him and for him.
- Hebrews 1:1-4: He is the fullness of God in bodily form.

Hebrews 1:3 (*AB*) reads: 'He is the sole expression of the glory of God [the Light-being, the out-raying or radiance of the divine], and he is the perfect imprint and very image of [God's] nature, upholding and maintaining and guiding and propelling the universe by his mighty word of power. When he had by offering himself accomplished our cleansing of sins and riddance of guilt, he sat down at the right hand of the divine Majesty on high.'

What a majestic image of Jesus! He upholds and propels the universe and atones for our sin.

Jesus, really God and really human, came to the earth to bring the presence of God in bodily form, to move into the neighbourhood, to live among us, even to become one of us. This is amazing. This is good news!

Our Lovesick God

One of the primary metaphors used to describe Jesus' relation to us, the Church, the people belonging to God, is that of a bridegroom. Take a look at these verses and listen to Jesus' heart of love for his people:

'Then, because so many people were coming and going that they did not even have a chance to eat, he said to them, "Come *with me* by yourselves to a quiet place and get some rest"' Mark 6:31 (our italics).

'Then he said to them, "My soul is overwhelmed with sorrow to the point of death. Stay here and keep watch *with me*"' Matthew 26:38 (our italics).

'And if I go and prepare a place for you, I will come back and take you to be *with me* that you also may be where I am' John 14:3 (our italics).

To the thief on the cross Jesus spoke words of love: 'Today you will be with me in paradise' (Luke 23:43).

In John 17:24 he prays: 'Father, I want those you have given me to be with me where I am, and to see my glory, the glory you have given me because you loved me before the creation of the world.'

In Matthew 8:20 we read: 'Jesus replied, "Foxes have holes. Birds of the air have nests. But the Son of Man has no place to lay his head"' (*New International Reader's Version*).

In contrast to some 'prosperity' teaching that mistakenly understands fullness in terms of wealth and worldly possessions, Jesus emphasizes his poverty and the transient nature of our life on earth.

Here is the climax of Jesus' 'high priestly prayer' in John 17:24-26: 'Father, I want those you have given me to be with me where I am, and to see my glory, the glory you have given me because you loved me before the creation of the world. Righteous Father, though the world does not know you, I know you, and they know that you have sent me. I have made you known to them, and will continue to make you known in order that the love you have for me may be in them and that I myself may be in them'.

Jesus wants us to love him like the Father loves him, that he may be in us. Jesus is committing to two initiatives towards two results: he is making the Father known to us and continuing to make him known to us; the Father's love for Jesus becomes ours and Jesus dwells in us.

How far will God go to make his home with us? All the way to death, even death on a cross.

A Holy Home for a Holy God: God in His People

The Glory and the Goodness

As you read through Exodus 33:18-20 and other passages, look for the relationship between the glory of God and the goodness of God.

Often we don't recognize the goodness of the Lord until it is in the past. We see it in hindsight:

- God's glory manifest in his goodness.
- When God's goodness is evident, so is God's glory.
- Look for and demonstrate God's goodness in your life. See his glory revealed in you.

The God Who Answers by Fire

'Then you call on the name of your god, and I will call on the name of the Lord. The god who answers by fire – he is God' (1 Kings 18:24). Fire…glory…presence.

Below are some biblical examples of God's presence as fire:

- Genesis 3:24 – cherubim hold *flaming* swords to guard Eden's entrance.
- Genesis 22:6-7 – at Abraham's sacrifice of Isaac.
- Exodus 12:8ff – the Mosaic covenant.
- Exodus 13:21ff – the pillar of fire and pillar of cloud.
- Exodus 19:18 – Mount Sinai.
- Leviticus 1:7; 6:9; Numbers 9:15 – fire in the Tabernacle.
- Leviticus 16:13 – the Day of Atonement.
- 2 Chronicles 7:1-3 – fire in the Temple.
- Acts 2:1-4 – there are tongues of fire at Pentecost, filling the house with fire.

Blood and Fire People: a Home for the God of Fire

We are people of the blood of Christ and people of the fire of the Holy

Spirit. Our God is a consuming fire. When God moves into the neighbourhood, he moves in as fire – and you are his neighbourhood.

'But who can endure the day of his coming? Who can stand when he appears? For he will be like a refiner's fire or a launderer's soap' (Malachi 3:2).

Beginning with William and Catherine Booth, The Salvation Army moved into its neighbourhoods, offering 'A place for those who have no place', a home for those who have no home. How far will we go to become God's home – to become holy? We must put aside all filthiness for us to become a holy home for a holy God. Individually and corporately, it is vital that we be the place where God dwells.

A Lesson from Acts

It can be said that there are two 'temples' in Acts chapter 2. One is the historic architectural structure in Jerusalem. The other 'temple' is the people, the pilgrims seeking God in Jerusalem at Pentecost, the day God came to dwell again with his people. God chose not the magnificent structure made of bricks, stones, curtains and altars, but rather the temples made of flesh and blood…the people.

Acts describes a transitional period in the dwelling place of God. The physical temple was doomed to be destroyed within a generation. But the believers were mobile and would spread to the ends of the earth once again as the dwelling place of God, taking the message of the gospel of Jesus Christ with them.

The homes in which believers met – settings replicated millions of times and in millions of places throughout history – provided a great model for a God who is on the move. Both 'temples' provided a gathering place for the faithful and the curious, but one was formal while the other was informal. One was transcendent while the other was intimate. One relied on ritual, the other on hospitality. One was fixed in place, the other was mobile and flexible. One was destined to become obsolete (along with other biblical symbols like the ark, the concept of 'devoted things', the golden serpent, circumcision and water baptism), the other was created for the fulfilment of the Great Commission.

This was not mere accident or serendipity. It was God's plan going back to Amos 9:11 at least. Jesus outlined the expansion plan in Acts 1:8 when he explained that the disciples would be transformed into witnesses by the power of the Holy Spirit and would spread from Jerusalem through Judea and Samaria to the ends of the earth. This pattern is characteristic of God. As Wesley Campbell says, 'Where God lands, God expands'. Pentecost was the next stage of this expansion. There were representatives of many nations present at Pentecost and thousands of them were saved. Most converts returned to their lands. They couldn't take a brick from the Temple home with them, but they could open themselves up as temples of the Holy Spirit. They could become homes for the living God – mobile homes, human hearts where God could move in and make himself at home.

According to Isaiah 57:15, God lives both in a high and holy place *and* with those who are contrite and lowly in spirit. The two temples to which we alluded in Acts chapter 2 are both represented here. The physical temple represents the high and holy place, while the people on the street on whom the Holy Spirit fell were the humble, the contrite and lowly in spirit. The inference we make, in light of the demolition of the physical temple is that God has now come to live among those who are humble – at least until the return of Jesus Christ, when it appears that God acquires a permanent new address: 'Now the dwelling of God is with men, and he will live with them' (Revelation 21:3 *NIV 1984*).

How is it that the King of Glory is described as standing at the door and knocking in Revelation 3:20? Could it be that he needs an invitation into his own prepared dwelling? Could it be that he is waiting for us to adopt a godly contrition for sins and a humble spirit – spiritual furniture that can accommodate his glory?

Surely we want more than visitation. We want habitation. Christ dwells in our hearts by faith (Ephesians 3:17). By faith let us exercise contrition and humility so that the Lord not only visits, but also inhabits our individual lives and our community of believers. This habitation is God's basis for prayer.

Bottom line: God announced that his house, the place where he dwells, would be a house of prayer. We must be that house.

The Dwelling Place of God

This diagram[39] offers a useful outline of the main ideas in this study:

The heavens and the earth
Garden of Eden
Abraham's family
Tabernacle
Temple
JESUS
Disciples
3,000 Jews
Jews and Gentiles
To the ends of the earth
The new heavens and the new earth

[36] Even when God came to earth in the flesh as the third person in the Godhead, the Lord Jesus Christ, he was homeless. Readers should understand that the term relates to the individual or group that has not yet submitted to him and welcomed him in. In relation to that individual or group, God remains homeless until he is invited to dwell in them.

[37] Jesus is truly and properly God and truly and properly man. That said, he was 'the man perfectly filled with (God the) Spirit' (see John Larsson, *The Man Perfectly Filled with the Spirit*, The Salvation Army, IHQ, 1986). Luke intimates that Jesus *and* John were filled with the Holy Spirit in the womb (see Luke 1:41).

[38] Yes, God is omnipresent, but he makes himself 'unipresent' through the Tabernacle, aiding a humanity grasping for the tangible.

[39] Major Noreen Batt, The Salvation Army, United Kingdom Territory with the Republic of Ireland.

Prayer Group Guide

• How can your praying community live out the truths of this teaching?

• What might help you to maintain your focus on God's incarnation?

• How can this teaching shape the prayers of your community?

• What is God initiating in your midst? How can you respond?

THE WAY FORWARD

SO there you have it: enough biblical and practical counsel to send you to your knees, aligned with God's will and well equipped to secure victory in Christ.

God is committed to a relationship with us – in fact, he is zealous to have a relationship with us. Our effective prayer must be grounded in relationship with God.

In writing this book, it wasn't our intention merely to add to the number of prayer manuals already lining Christians' bookshelves. Our goal has been to communicate principles that would infuse our readers' daily lives with new disciplines and new levels of freedom. Whether we achieve that goal, however, is up to you.

We'll hazard a tired (but apt) cliché by declaring that this is not the end, but the beginning – the beginning of a faith-filled, devoted, confident, obedient fight, a fight we hope you'll now enter with renewed resolve.

Our prayer is that you'll receive at least some of our words as words from God and that they'll help transform you into a mighty warrior for Jesus Christ. Think of each lesson as a piece of armour. It is armour that will make you stronger and more effective in the great salvation war.

What remains, then, is to 'fight the good fight.' So, as General Paul Rader once exhorted The Salvation Army:

'Let's go forward – on our knees!'

RESOURCES

THE following have either been mentioned in this book or are recommended as excellent resources:

Websites
www.24-7prayer.com
www.armybarmy.com
www.armyonitsknees.org
www.blueletterbible.org
www.ccel.org
www.ihop.org
www.saglobal247.org
www.salvationarmyspirituallife.org
http://sar.my/intpray
www.saytunes.com

Books/Publications

- Judith Bennett, *White Cloud Soaring*, Flag Publications, The Salvation Army, 2009.
- Mike Bickle with Dana Candler, *The Rewards of Fasting*, Forerunner Media, 2005.
- Dietrich Bonhoeffer, *Life Together*, SCM Press, 1954.
- Catherine Booth, *The Highway of Our God: Selections from the Army Mother's Writings*, The Salvation Army, SP&S, 1954.
- Catherine Booth, *Papers on Godliness. Being Reports on a Series of Addresses Delivered at St James's Hall, London, During 1881*, The Salvation Army, International Headquarters, 1890.
- William Booth, *The Seven Spirits: Or, What I Teach My Officers*, The Salvation Army Book Department, 1907.
- Samuel Logan Brengle, *Heart Talks on Holiness*, The Salvation Army, SP&S, 1915.
- Samuel Logan Brengle, *Helps to Holiness*, The Salvation Army, SP&S, 1896.
- Wesley and Stacey Campbell, *Praying the Bible: the Book of Prayers* and *Praying the Bible: the Pathway to Spirituality*, Regal Books, 2002 and 2003.

• Mahesh Chavda, *The Hidden Power of Prayer and Fasting*, Destiny Image Publishers, 1998.
• Richard Foster, *Celebration of Discipline: The Path to Spiritual Growth*, Hodder & Stoughton, 2008.
• Richard Foster, *Prayer: Finding the Heart's True Home*, Hodder & Stoughton, 2008.
• James Garlow, *The Covenant: A Study of God's Extraordinary Love for You*, Beacon Hill Press, 1999.
• Edmund Gosse and William Penn, *Some Fruits of Solitude in Reflection and Maxims*, Kessinger Publishing, 2010.
• John Gowans, *O Lord!*, The Salvation Army, SP&S, 1981.
• Pete Greig, *God on Mute: Engaging the Silence of Unanswered Prayer*, Kingsway Books, 2007.
• Pete Greig, *Red Moon Rising*, Kingsway Publications, 2004.
• Tony Jones, *The Sacred Way*, Zondervan, 2005.
• *Journal of Aggressive Christianity*, visit www.armybarmy.com
• Sunder Krishnan, *The Conquest of Inner Space: Learning the Language of Prayer*, WingSpread Publishers (originally published by Scarlet Cord Press, 2003).
• John Larsson, *The Man Perfectly Filled With the Spirit*, IHQ, 1986.
• Beth Moore, *A Woman's Heart: God's Dwelling Place*, Lifeway Christian Resources, 1995.
• Phil Needham, *Community in Mission: a Salvationist Ecclesiology*, The Salvation Army, 1987.
• Eugene Peterson, *Reversed Thunder: The Revelation of John and the Praying Imagination*, Harper Collins, 1988.
• Bruce Power, *Conversations with God*, The Salvation Army, Canada and Bermuda Territory, 2005.
• Dutch Sheets, *Intercessory Prayer*, Regal Books, 2009.
• Elmer Towns, *Fasting for Spiritual Breakthrough: A Guide to Nine Biblical Fasts*, Regal Books, 1996.
• Hannah Whitall Smith, *The Christian's Secret of a Happy Life*, Whitaker House Books, 1983.
• Dallas Willard, *The Spirit of the Disciplines: Understanding How God Changes Lives (Audiobook)*, Hodder & Stoughton, 1996.

APPENDIX

An invitation – Worldwide Prayer Meeting

One Army, One Mission, One Message

Mission statement of the international Centre for Spiritual Life Development

A call to prayer and mission

An invitation – Worldwide Prayer Meeting

On 1 September 2011, the international leader of The Salvation Army, General Linda Bond, offered this open invitation to join her in weekly prayer.

EVERY Thursday, The Salvation Army around the world is in prayer for the entire day. Territories, commands and individual Salvationists have signed up, covenanting to use 30 minutes each Thursday between 5.00am and 8.00am to pray for the Army – its zeal for God, its compassionate service in every community and its daring and fruitful witness to the gospel of Jesus Christ.

Driven by a desire to be the people God wants us to be and to do what he wants us to do, we commit ourselves to seeking the only One who can empower us with the Holy Spirit and energise and equip us for ministry in the 21st century.

One officer has written to me, 'Some corps and divisional headquarters have changed their regular weekly prayer time to Thursday so more and more of us are lifting our requests to God at the same time. I've just come from the territorial headquarters prayer meeting where one pray-er likened this worldwide prayer meeting to a "Mexican wave" making its way around the globe as Thursday dawns in each new place – that's one massive Mexican wave which God will not ignore.'

May the Lord hear the prayers of the tens of thousands of Salvationists united in seeking him.

The Vision Plan on the following pages outlines the Vision Statement of 'One Army, One Mission, One Message' and includes the 12 International Mission Priorities launched on Thursday 13 October 2011. The priorities are headed by a determined 'we will'.

Let's pray through the vision. Let's pray specifically for each Mission Priority. Dwell on each phrase in the Vision Statement and in each priority. Explore what they mean for you personally as well as for your corps/centre, division, command/territory and for the Army internationally.

Begin with praise and thanksgiving, for we have been a blessed people, and a blessing, since he called the Army into being almost 150 years ago. Then let's move to confession – where we have failed him – possibly because we have been more concerned about our own image and self-preservation than the winning of the lost. Let's petition and intercede so that we will be found faithful in holy living, sanctified activism and fruitful ministry. Let's offer ourselves afresh for him to use his Army for his will and purpose in the 21st century.

Locally your territory/command may be using different language or terminology when it comes to mission and vision, but at the heart of it all is being faithful as his people in his service.

So together, let's praise, confess, ask and surrender to him to see Spirit-inspired and Spirit-blessed action.

May the Lord be honoured and glorified as we unite in prayer.

Yours sincerely,

Linda Bond
General

One Army, One Mission, One Message

ONE ARMY
A God-raised, Spirit-filled
Army for the 21st century
convinced of its calling
moving forward together

ONE MISSION
into the world
of the hurting, broken,
lonely, dispossessed and lost,
reaching them in love
by all means

ONE MESSAGE
with the transforming message
of Jesus,
bringing freedom,
hope and life.

Vision Plan

ONE ARMY
We see a God-raised, Spirit-filled Army for the 21st century – convinced of our calling, moving forward together
ONE MISSION
Into the world of the hurting, broken, lonely, dispossessed and lost, reaching them in love by all means
ONE MESSAGE
With the transforming message of Jesus, bringing freedom, hope and life
THE SALVATION ARMY
WE WILL ...
deepen our spiritual life
unite in prayer
identify and develop leaders
increase self-support and self-denial
WE WILL ...
emphasise our integrated ministry
reach and involve youth and children
stand for and serve the marginalised
encourage innovation in mission
WE WILL ...
communicate Christ unashamedly
reaffirm our belief in transformation
evangelise and disciple effectively
provide quality teaching resources

CSLD

centre for spiritual life development

Mission statement of the international Centre for Spiritual Life Development

The international Centre for Spiritual Life Development exists to facilitate the development of the spiritual lives of Salvationists by:

- Offering **conferences and events** that are spiritually enriching and that help form people in Christlikeness
- Providing **resources** to cultivate spiritual life development
- Encouraging implementation of **intentional and systematic opportunities** for spiritual growth throughout the international Salvation Army.

www.salvationarmyspirituallife.org

A call to prayer and mission

GOD is calling our Army to prayer! He is calling us to urgent, prevailing prayer for the renewal of our love for Christ, a recommitment to our spiritual priorities in mission, and a clearer vision of his purpose for the Army as we approach the year 2000.

The Salvation war in which we are engaged is real. The enemy against whom we fight is powerful. But he is not invincible. Indeed, he was defeated at the Cross and exposed to open shame (Colossians 2:15). Still, the battle rages on. Never has the conflict been more intense. Never has there been a greater need for prayer.

We rejoice in every evidence of a revival of prayer in our ranks – and beyond: prayer fellowship, prayer vigils, prayer marches, prayer support teams for musical sections, schools of prayer, nights of prayer, concerts of prayer and much more. In 100 countries around our globe the voices of Salvationists in prayer ascend to the throne of grace every hour, day and night. We are a praying Army. But let us confess that for all too many of us, prayer may quickly become a lifeless routine, an empty and powerless ritual, if it is not neglected altogether.

Let every Salvationist take a personal inventory of the place, priority and power of prayer in his or her own life. Do I have a regular time for personal and family worship and prayer? What is the place of prayer in our planning and programmes at our corps and centres? When do we pray? Who prays? With what expectation? With what result? Is God calling some of us to a specific ministry of intercession or spiritual warfare through prayer?

As General of The Salvation Army, I am asking that every Salvationist and every centre of Army activity consider making a specific commitment to prayer for the next 12 months. The nature of that commitment should be negotiated personally with the Holy Spirit. I seek a commitment beyond our present routines. Let prayer be more disciplined, more specific, more consistent.

For what, then, shall we pray?

• Pray for peace and an end to tribal and ethnic violence, while confessing our own failure to be instruments of his peace. Ask God where we ourselves might bring healing as his ambassadors of reconciliation (2 Corinthians 5:18-20) – in our homes, our marriages, our corps, our communities.

• Pray for unity among us, the two or three together in his name, and as a global force for salvation and healing of the nations – partners in mission.

• Pray for the salvation of the lost – for a new spirit of holy aggression in our evangelism.

• Pray for world evangelisation – the salvation of the unreached peoples of earth, according to 'the command of the eternal God, so that all nations might believe and obey him' (Romans 16:26 *NIV 1984*).

• Pray for the growth of the Army in spiritual depth and devotion. Pray for new corps and new people, 'brought out of the dominion of darkness and into the Kingdom of the Son he loves' (General Rader, based on Colossians 1:13).

• Pray that God will raise up an Army of senior soldiers, women and men, a million strong, around the world, marching under the one flag.

• Pray for Army leaders – for vision, grace and courage. Pray for them not just as leaders, but also as vulnerable human persons.

• Pray for the confusion and defeat of all the stratagems of Satan and for the deliverance of those held captive to his will.

• Pray for the salvation and moral protection of our young people, for a love for the Word of God, courage to stand for Christ, and a willingness to give radical obedience to his will.

• Pray for officer candidates, lay volunteers, and those

who in midlife will put their skills and experience at God's disposal.

• Pray for our Army's worldwide ministries of helping, healing and wholeness among the sick, the powerless, and the poorest of the poor.

• Pray for children caught in the crossfire of war, the homeless, brutalized and abandoned.

• Pray for the beauty of the Lord our God to be upon us as a movement – the beauty of his holiness (Psalm 90:17).

• Pray for a new appreciation of our royal privilege of coming to God at his invitation, for a daily audience with our Saviour King, 'that we may receive mercy and find grace to help us in our time of need' (Hebrews 4:16).

• Pray that a Spirit-inspired movement of prayer reaching the throne of God will bring a mighty tidal wave of salvation blessing sweeping over our Army around the world, a tsunami of the spirit, cleansing, refreshing and renewing us for mission.

• Pray that Jesus Christ will be glorified through this his Army.

On our knees, let us look again at our own homes, our communities, and our world, careering out of control toward the next century. If you believe with me that God is calling his Army to prayer, then decide now to do something about it – and do it now, for Jesus' sake, and for the salvation of the world for which he died. Let us go forward – on our knees!

General Paul A. Rader
Westminster Central Hall,
London, November 1994

Called To Be God's People

Robert Street

The work of the International Spiritual Life Commission (ISLC) has brought much benefit to Salvationists, not least through the writings of Commissioner Robert Street. This 2008 book is a revised edition of his 1999 volume of the same name, and brings greater clarity to the issues in light of experience since the original publication. The book uses the 12 Calls of the ISLC as its framework, offering clear, concise teaching for groups or individuals. Also available as a DVD.

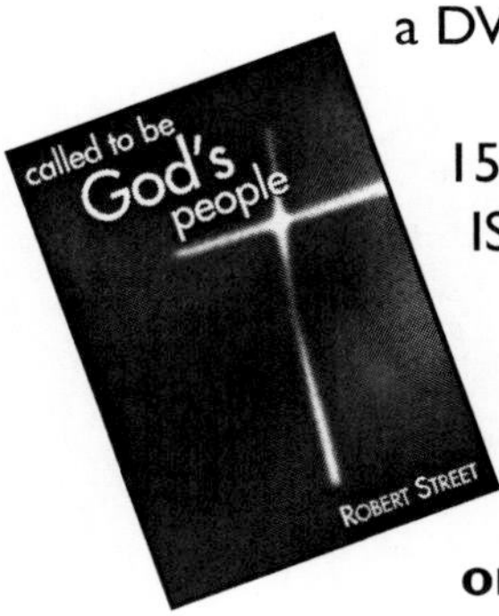

156pp (paperback)
ISBN 978-0-85412-786-3

Can be purchased from any Salvation Army trade or supplies department and online at www.amazon.co.uk

Called To Preach – Sermons by Salvationist Women

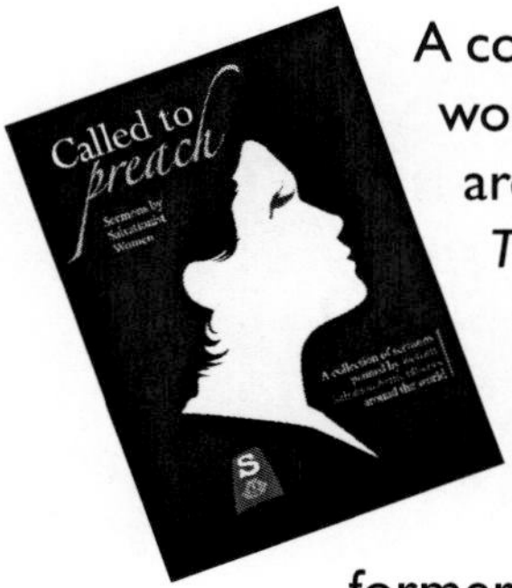

A collection of 35 sermons penned by women Salvation Army officers from around the world and including *The Times* 2000 'Preacher of the Year' award-winning 'The People Who Walked in Darkness Have Seen a Great Light', by Colonel Margaret Hay. An initiative of former World President of Women's Ministries, Commissioner Helen Clifton, this book is dedicated to her memory as she was promoted to Glory shortly before its publication.

208pp (paperback)
ISBN 978-0-85412-839-6

Can be purchased from any Salvation Army trade or supplies department and online at www.amazon.co.uk

Love – Right at the Heart

Robert Street

Written in harmony with General Linda Bond's call – One Army, One Mission, One Message – this book examines how Christians have a responsibility to one another, whilst taking their caring ministry to the world. Through Sam and Joe's informal 'After the meeting' sessions and a subsequent 'Heart to heart' section, each aspect of love is considered in the context of day-to-day service.

144pp (paperback)
ISBN 978-0-85412-841-9

Can be purchased from any Salvation Army trade or supplies department and online at www.amazon.co.uk